EVERYTHING YOU NEED TO KNOW ABOUT

WHISKY

(but are too afraid to ask)

EVERYTHING YOU NEED TO KNOW ABOUT

WHISKY

(but are too afraid to ask)

NICHOLAS MORGAN

THE WHISKY
EXCHANGE

EBURY
PRESS

INTRODUCTION

When I was initially asked about doing a whisky book, my simple answer was, no, there were so many good whisky books out there already. However, once our friends at Ebury explained that they didn't want just another whisky guide, and that we could choose with them who we wanted to write the book, I realised this was an opportunity to do something different.

I wanted us to write about all the aspects of whisky that we discuss every day at The Whisky Exchange and over drams when we meet up with friends. The debates, the myths, the whiskies that inspire us, who we admire and what we'd like to change if we could. We couldn't think of any other book which helped whisky lovers navigate these waters, so my 'no' swiftly changed to a 'yes'.

Having been pretty much born into the drinks business and seen things from both a collector's and retailer's viewpoint, I wanted to balance our point of view with someone who came from a different side of the industry. I wanted someone to look at things from both a brand owner's and enthusiast's perspective, and of course someone who could write eloquently and really knew what they were talking about.

I first met Nick Morgan at an auction in the early 1990s when he was the archivist at United Distillers. Obviously, we were bidding on the same bottles. Nick has been involved with every aspect of the whisky industry and has been behind the launch and promotion of many of the successful Diageo malts. He has a strategic and methodological approach to things while always having the long-term interest of whisky at the heart of everything he does. He has been a mentor to many of the younger and more prominent writers and bloggers of today. He has always taken an interest in The Whisky Exchange and he has been a valuable industry colleague and friend. We have had many interesting conversations about whisky over the years, disagreeing on many occasions but always in a healthy and respectful way. In my mind Nick was the only person to write this book.

Most whisky authors write about the romance of whisky, making people buy into the product and the tradition that goes with it. We wanted to take a deeper look into the issues around whisky and the myths that have become part of its history. The things you believed to be true that might not be so. So in this book we present the different sides of the argument, led of course by Nick's inimitable take on things; the aim is to stimulate debate, to leave you pondering over what you believe, and inspire you to pour a glass of your favourite whisky while you mull it all over. In many cases, there is no right or wrong answer.

This is a book for anyone who loves whisky. They don't have to be experts, far from it, and there will be plenty to discover (and reconsider) for even the most impassioned and well-informed whisky fan. We delve into where flavour comes from – is it production or maturation? What is the history and importance of the wood that is used to age whisky? How does the world of whisky work outside Scotland? Is whisky just a science? Does the concept of terroir in whisky exist? We look at how whisky has played a part in different countries and cultures around the world and its social and cultural impact. We examine the importance of

Rajbir and Sukhinder Singh, founders of The Whisky Exchange.

∧

whisky blends, and how they took whisky to the masses making it the global force we know today. We look at the collapse and renaissance of Irish whiskey and Prohibition in the US, how drinking habits have changed and the growth of single malts and world whisky.

We are reminded that whisky is a business at the end of the day. Companies need to make a profit to survive and will sometimes do whatever is necessary to achieve this. Companies merge, they take over competitors, they increase profits by making efficiencies, and new companies enter the fray to challenge them and try to take a share of their business. Whisky is very much an economic story as well as a romantic one, and that story is told here.

We wanted to create a book that asked (and hopefully answers) the questions every whisky lover ponders. How does the world drink whisky? Are there any rules? Does anyone care? Is the glass important? What about the culture of mixing and adding ice or water? Who are the real whisky experts and who are the charlatans?

Whisky is about trying different styles and bottles. With hundreds of new releases each year, we never stop learning. I have gained good experience and knowledge over the last forty-plus years, but I don't consider myself an expert. I simply try to share the knowledge I have with others to help them on their whisky journey as many of my peers did with me. Everyone is obsessed with single malts – and often for good reason – but one thing I like about this book is that it reminds us that at the end of the day everything is a blend.

Today, whisky collecting is a popular hobby where demand outstrips supply for most limited releases. This has created a

Above all, whisky is about people and stories.

speculative market that has been lucrative for many over the last few years. We cover this area too as there is a very little guidance about it, and we wanted to provide a bit of enlightenment. We discover that collecting is actually a form of illness, and after 35 years of collecting, (un)fortunately, it is too late for me to be cured.

Above all, whisky is about people and stories. From the beginning we wanted to make sure this played a significant part in this book. Who are the people that made whisky what it is today? A hundred years ago and before, there were the whisky barons who travelled the world promoting their brands, the writers that wrote about the science of whisky and differences between the hundreds of distilleries. As whisky has become popular over the last 20 years, today we look towards the ambassadors, the bloggers and multitude of books that have been written. Through my whisky journey I have had the privilege to meet many unique and inspiring characters, spending time with them, hearing old stories and anecdotes over long evenings accompanied by good food and fine whisky.

The book has reminded me how the industry has changed and developed, the challenges it has faced and that all is not what we read in books and hear from people who work in it today. It is not that they are wrong but there is always an additional story to tell. When I started collecting, there were not many like-minded enthusiasts to share my passion with. I have seen so much change over the years and have had virtually every rare bottle through my hands at some time or other. I have been fortunate enough to try nearly every whisky expression that has been released over the last two decades. My heroes in most part are retired or have passed away. I am now old in terms of my time in the industry and people look up to me like I did to them. I must continue the journey that my peers started, passing on stories to the next generation of drinkers. I hope that I might even be remembered in books like this in years to come.

— Sukhinder Singh

HOW WHISKY
IS MADE

01

'It is surprising how little knowledge
of the process of manufacture of Scotch
whisky is possessed by the many thousands
of its consumers throughout the world.
It is especially surprising when one
reflects that, if only these individuals
could follow its production, as it were
through a Brobdingnagian microscope,
capable of bringing under the eye at once
comprehensively, but in detail, the whole
commercial process, he would marvel at
the wonderful natural agencies harnessed
to the service of the producer.'

— Stuart Hastie, *From Burn to Bottle*, 1921

This first chapter will guide you through the myriad complexities of the whisky-making process, and introduce some of the arcane language used to describe the various stages and critical equipment used. After all, mastering the language is almost as important as understanding the science; it is a passport to the inner sanctum of the whisky enthusiast. Curious scientists, distiller's desires to control every aspect of production and increasingly complicated kit for measuring each stage of the process might make the process seem riddled with complexities, but making whisky is actually very simple. And to be honest, it's something probably best understood by visiting a distillery; this is where the sights, smells and even sudden changes in temperature give a visceral explanation of the process. It's something that's been going on in Scotland for well over 500 years. While our understanding of the science of whisky has increased enormously during this time, the actual making of it is still more or less as it would have been in 1494 when Friar John Cor (a monk of very uncertain origins) received the famous command from James IV of Scotland to take 'eight bolls of malt to make *aqua vitae*'. This posh Latin phrase, '*aqua vitae*', or 'the water of life', transformed into the Scots Gaelic 'uisge-beatha' after the dissolution of the monasteries, and then conveniently from simply 'uisqe' to 'whisky' and was the product of the same simple conversion process that goes on today. In the coming pages, we'll explore this conversion process, and the way whisky is distilled around the world, from Scotland and Ireland, to America and even Japan. Each country has their own take on the process, with huge implications for the flavour of the final product. And we'll see that while whisky making is a science, it is also an art and its secrets remain shrouded in mystery.

SINGLE MALT SCOTCH WHISKY

Single malt Scotch is made from malted barley and distilled in a batch process in copper pot stills at a single distillery.

∧

The production of whisky in Scotland is closely regulated by law and there are three main types of whisky made here: single malt Scotch, single grain Scotch and blended Scotch. Single malt is made from malted barley and distilled in a batch process in pot stills in a single distillery. Single grain is made from a mixture of malted barley and maize or wheat, and distilled in a continuous process in a Coffey or patent still, again in a single distillery. Finally, blended Scotch is made by mixing several (often many) single malt Scotch whiskies together with single grain Scotch whiskies. Blending is a subject we will return to later (see page 47), but for the record more than 90 per cent of all the Scotch whisky that's sold globally is blended Scotch. Well-informed readers will observe that, when it comes to publicity, single malts consistently dominate the Scotch whisky conversation. In reality, single malt Scotches makes up less than 10 per cent of sales.

BARLEY AND MALT

Barley is the main ingredient of single malt Scotch whisky. The conversion process begins with malting, once carried out at individual distilleries but now, save for a few instances where old methods are retained to please tourists, conducted in large industrial facilities that service a number of makers. A misty-eyed nostalgia surrounds old-style 'floor maltings', where barley would be laid out on long floors to germinate, the grain regularly 'turned' by workers with large wooden shovels. Photographs of floor maltings still frequently feature in books and articles about Scotch, which rarely mention the injurious effect that 'turning malt' had on the health of those who drew the short straw for a shift with the malt shovel. Malting was never the exact science that some would like to imagine; the old floor maltings were hugely inefficient and inconsistent in the quality of malt they delivered. In the quest for greater efficiency and consistency, some malt whisky distilleries, such as Glen Grant and Speyburn, started using large, pneumatic malting equipment from the end of the nineteenth century. More technology was gradually introduced until the majority of floor maltings were abandoned in the 1960s and 1970s. Repetitive strain injuries, sometimes called 'monkey shoulder', and respiratory conditions provoked by the high levels of dust and deposit in the atmosphere meant few mourned their passing.

As with distilling itself, malting is very simple. Regardless of the time of year, the maltster's job is to encourage the barley seed to think it's spring and persuade it to grow by soaking the grain in large vessels or steeps. It is then left to germinate before growth is stopped by drying the grain with a heat source. During this mini-growing season the structure of the barley seed is modified to ensure that its starches and proteins are in a form suitable to provide the right amount of extract needed by the distiller. Ultimately the test of a good malted barley rests on the amount of alcohol it delivers. Although all malt whiskies possess a cereal or malty character, individual varieties of barley actually play little part in delivering specific flavour characteristics to the final matured whisky, despite some distillers' claims to the contrary. At this early stage of the process, efficiency and yield are key, and it is the accountant, not the distiller, who calls the shots. There is, of course, one exception to this generalisation – indeed, we will find that in whisky making there is always at least one exception to every hard and fast rule. In some maltings the heat source used to arrest the germination process includes peat; decayed, decomposed and dried vegetation that when burnt delivers a distinctive phenolic, or smoky, character to the malted barley that is carried all the way through the subsequent parts of the process. Although now most associated with coastal or island malt whisky distilleries in Scotland, peat was at one time used in the kilns of the majority of distilleries, and Scotch's reputation was forged around the world in the nineteenth century by its characteristic smoky goût.

This distinctive character is still produced by open peat fires that drive smoke through the drying malted barley and, as such, the peating process is the most difficult to control. Distillers have exacting specifications for the phenolic content of the malt they use, measured by PPMs (phenolic parts per million), but these are often only achieved by blending together various batches of malt with differing peating levels to reach the desired number. Even then it is not the phenolic content of a particular batch of malt that guarantees the smokiness of the final mature whisky, but the interventions of the distiller. Famously the Lagavulin and Caol lla distilleries on Islay use malt produced at the island's Port Ellen maltings to the same phenolic specifications – yet the whiskies they produce are entirely different in terms of their smokiness. Some malt whisky enthusiasts are transfixed by PPMs, always looking for the biggest number and their next hit. In whisky culture, where the appreciation of extremes is often mistaken for knowledge or connoisseurship, some go in search of the smokiest whisky, as if on a quest to find the hottest curry after a night of indiscriminate beer drinking.

Barley, sometimes but not always grown in Scotland, is the main ingredient of single malt Scotch whisky.

∧

> Although all malt whiskies possess a cereal or malty character, individual varieties of barley actually play little part in delivering specific flavour characteristics to the final matured whisky, despite some distillers' claims to the contrary.

MILLING AND MASHING

Next on to the process of milling and mashing. Once the malt has been delivered to the distillery it has to be milled into a coarse mixture called grist, which is broken down into three parts: husk, grits and flour; the proportions of which vary from distillery to distillery. A shoogly box, a device made up of three horizontal sieves, which separates the three elements in the grist when shaken (or 'shoogled'), is still used alongside modern equipment to determine whether the proportions are correct. Most Scottish distilleries proudly boast of the age of the brightly painted mills that visitors see, though they are not neccesarily the mills they really use. The majority of these mills were built by one of two English companies: Richard Sizer of Hull (Porteus mills) and Robert Boby of Bury St Edmunds (the eponymous Boby mills). Neither are made today, both having failed to grasp that some degree of built-in obsolescence would ensure a continued market for their products.

From the mill, the grist then passes to the mash tun. Mash tuns were once large cast-iron vessels with mechanical rakes circulating to stir the porridge-like mixture created by adding hot water to the grist, but are now usually made of stainless steel with lauter technology borrowed from the brewing industry used to increase the extract from the malt. During this process, the starches in the malt are converted to fermentable sugars. Each batch of grist is subjected to two increasingly hot waters that will be sent on to the next stage, while a final third of water is retained to become the first water of the next batch. The residue of this process, the remnants of the milled grist, or draff, rich in proteins is a traditional form of animal feed, sometimes collected from distilleries by local farmers, now more often than not processed into pelleted form using other liquid by-products of the distilling process. Draff is also increasingly used for bio-energy production.

YEAST AND FERMENTATION

The sugary liquid that results from the mashing process, known as wort, is cooled and then passed to the tun room where the fermentation process takes place. Only one distillery, the tiny Edradour in Perthshire, still uses the late Victorian cooling method, a Morton's Refrigerator, a shallow metal tank filled with cold water that the wort passes through in narrow tubes. Most distilleries now choose to use modern heat exchangers. Large wooden tuns normally made from Oregon pine or larch, known as washbacks, are used to ferment the wort to produce wash, effectively a beer of around 8 per cent alcohol by volume. Some believe that the washbacks play an essential role in developing spirit character or flavour, although the choice of pine and larch is based purely on the size of the tree, and the impervious nature of its wood. Some distillers use stainless-steel washbacks, claiming they are more hygienic. Others, like Diageo, although sometimes happy to use stainless steel in new builds or distillery extensions, have never replaced wooden washbacks with stainless steel. As we shall see later, distillers can be remarkably conservative, afraid any change might lead to a change in the quality of the whisky they produce.

Yeast is added to the wort and so the sugars are converted to alcohol; often distillers will choose to use a mixture of commercially produced distiller's yeast and brewer's yeast, recovered from the beer-making process, either in solid or liquid form. In addition to these it's probable that naturally occurring yeasts specific to each distillery also play a role in the fermentation, despite the strict hygiene regimes in place to ensure there is no contamination. The development of flavour congeners, a by-product of the alcohol conversion process that does much to determine the character of the spirit, is a critical part of this stage, which can continue after the yeasts are exhausted and the maximum amount of alcohol produced. The length of the fermentation is a significant factor in determining the flavour characteristics of the final spirit and mature whisky. A short fermentation, say around 48 hours, would normally produce a spirit with what distillers would call a 'nutty spicy' character. Longer fermentations – in some distilleries they can be over a hundred hours – allow more complex fruity flavours to emerge. Much of this is believed to be due to the presence of lactobacilli, bacteria that help to develop flavour. Fermenting wort was once popular as a mid-shift refreshment for distillery workers, with the nickname 'badger' or 'Joe', sweet, mildly alcoholic and known for having an almost immediate and frankly quite devastating effect on the bowels.

DISTILLATION

The final stage in the conversion process sees the wash converted to spirit, normally through a two-stage batch distillation process. Simple though it may be, this part is over-burdened with a painful degree of distiller's jargon. Stills are large copper vessels in which fermented wort is boiled in order to produce spirit from the condensed vapours. Copper pot stills normally operate in pairs, so a distillery might have two, or four, or six, or even twenty-eight. Very occasionally, and unusually, a distillery might have an odd number of stills, like Talisker on the Isle of Skye, which has five. An odd number of stills normally suggests an unorthodox distillation regime, which may well deliver a specific spirit character. The first still in each pair is the wash or low-wines still, the second is the spirit still. We'll talk a bit more about stills and copper later (see page 22), but for now you just need to know that each still has a lyne arm (or lye pipe – why have one name when you can have two?) which runs from the head or neck of the still to the condenser, which might be a shell and tube condenser or a 'worm'. (We'll explain the difference between these two types of condensers shortly.) The wash passes from the wash charger to the wash still, where it is boiled. The majority of distilleries use a steam coil at the base of the still to heat the wash – some, like Glenfiddich, still use 'direct fired' stills, with gas replacing the traditional coal. The resulting vapours pass up the still and along the lyne arm to the condenser where they are converted back to liquid, known as low wines, at around 20 per cent alcohol by volume (abv). This spirit passes through a spirit safe to the low-wines receiver. The spirit safe, normally a gleaming copper and glass structure, is where the stillman chooses which spirit to keep from any batch. During the second distillation in the spirit still, which is normally smaller than the wash still, the stillman will select the 'middle cut' of the spirit which will be kept for maturation. The foreshots (the early run of spirit before the cut point) and the feints (the spirit that flows after the middle cut has been taken) are retained and added to the low wines and feints charger for the next distillation. Like an expanding and shrinking waistline the 'middle cut' can vary enormously between distilleries, each one choosing the very precise part of the run that will deliver the exact character the distiller is seeking. The residue from the distillation process, the pot ale and spent lees, can be combined with draff from the mash tun as animal feed or fuel, or used by farmers as a liquid fertiliser.

A simple conversion process: from barley to spirit, but not yet all the way to Scotch. By law the new make spirit must be filled into oak casks and matured in Scotland for a minimum of three years before it can officially be called Scotch whisky. A more detailed look at wood and the maturation process follows later in our journey (see page 54), but suffice to say here that for all the interventions the distiller may make during distillation to influence the character of the spirit, the greatest intervention, and most profound conversion, takes place when the spirit meets the wood. Views may differ, but under normal circumstances the interaction of spirit, wood and time accounts for around 70 per cent of the flavour development in the whisky.

The malt whisky making process, from malting, milling and mashing through to fermenting, distillation and, finally, maturation.

>

THE COPPER CONVERSATION

The 'distillery character' of the new make spirit is critical in determining how the whisky finally tastes and many distillers go to great lengths to ensure that this unique character shines through in the mature spirit, rather than being overwhelmed by wood effect. But what are the elements in the conversion process that really do determine distillery character? We've already seen that the use of peat to dry malted barley can have a major impact on flavour. The variety of barley, once a key selling point for at least one major single malt whisky brand, is now much less so, if at all. The deeply cherished belief that the water source impacts on the taste, much beloved by directors of the now lamented whisky films of the 1980s, is now largely discredited. Water is critical: distillers need good clean water free of nitrates to make whisky, and they need a lot of water to help move the process along, but it is not a factor in flavour formulation. Really, the front end of the conversion process is all about efficiency and extract, and matters of flavour begin with fermentation. Yeast is a critical component here and it is the subject of much experimentation, partly around the efficiency with which strains of yeast convert sugars to alcohol, and partly around the flavours different yeasts can produce. Pombe yeast (which has a very complicated and long scientific name of the sort that whisky enthusiasts love to memorise) was trialled at Glen Elgin distillery on Speyside a number of years ago, and produced a profoundly distinct new make spirit with the character of green apples. However, as the experimental spirit was matured it became apparent that this new make character significantly diminished. Nonetheless many new small distilleries, who are all fighting to create a distinctive and unique selling point for their brands, are revisiting yeast strains as one route to standing out among the (very busy) crowd.

The engine of flavour production has to be the still room, where numerous variables offer the distiller almost limitless options to determine what spirit character they want. The magic and mystery of the still room resides in the copper pot stills, and in what former Lagavulin and Royal Lochnagar distillery manager Mike Nicolson famously dubbed, the 'copper conversation'. Pot stills come in all shapes and sizes, from tiny (like those at Royal Lochnagar or Edradour) to huge (at Glenkinchie near Edinburgh or the recently built Dalmunach on Speyside). They are normally handcrafted by coppersmiths at a small number of companies in Scotland, although the recent increase in small start-up distilleries has seen some employ less conventional and certainly less attractive stills made on the continent as demand outstrips supply. Each distillery is proud and protective of the shape of its stills; change the shape, so the saying goes, and you change the whisky. Although each distillery's stills are unique, there are three main styles or shapes: a plain still, a ball still and a lamp-glass still. The shape and height of the still are important in determining the amount of reflux that occurs during the distillation process, that is to say, the number of times that vapours return to liquid and are

Patent stills and pot stills. Most malt whisky distilleries distil in two copper pot stills. Traditionally grain whisky distilleries use patent or Coffey stills to produce their whiskies, a form of distillation that was introduced in 1830 and first used at Cameronbridge distillery in Fife.

⌄

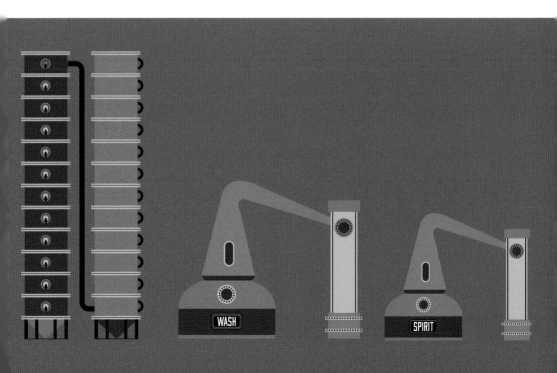

redistilled before passing over the swan neck at the head of the still into the lyne arm and on to the condenser. The amount of reflux determines the intensity of the copper conversation, or the amount of contact between copper and spirit vapours. Copper is a natural purifier and it strips out heavier sulphury elements in the spirit vapours. The more intense the conversation in the still, the lighter the spirit character produced. Time and temperature all add to the nature of this discussion. Everything about a still room set-up is about this interaction. Not just the stills' shape and size, but also the angle of the lyne arm and the type of condensers used. The shell and tube condenser, a late Victorian innovation, where the spirit vapours pass over small copper tubes of cold water delivers a relatively fast, intense condensation. In the more traditional worm tubs, relatively few of which are used in Scotland today, the vapours travel through a single coiled copper pipe, wide at the top, narrow at the bottom, which sits in a wooden or metal tub, filled with cooling water. This results in a very minimal copper exposure, the result being a heavier spirit, sometimes with a distinct

A copper pot still with a traditional worm condenser produces an old fashioned heavier style of malt whisky.

∨

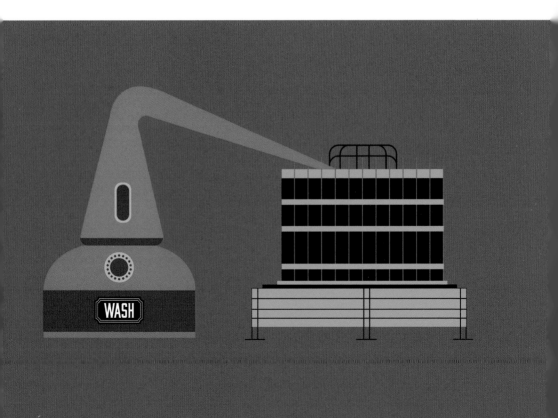

sulphur character, often described as 'meaty'. Although they might not sound too appetising, these old-fashioned worm-tub whiskies are highly prized for the very unique characters they produce when mature. One of the most revered is Mortlach, from a distillery with a bewilderingly complex arrangement of stills and worms. Another spectacle to behold are the horseshoe-shaped lyne arms over the worm tubs at Talisker distillery. Condensers are normally situated inside the still house, worms are outside, and therefore also at the mercy of the changing temperature from season to season.

SINGLE GRAIN SCOTCH WHISKY

Much of what is written above in terms of the basic conversion process also applies to the production of grain whisky in Scotland. The principle difference between grain whisky production and malt whisky production is the size and scale of grain whisky distilleries, the raw materials they use and the type of stills employed. Traditionally grain whisky distilleries use patent or Coffey stills to produce their whiskies, a form of distillation that was introduced in 1830 and first used at Cameronbridge distillery in Fife. At Girvan distillery, William Grant's produce grain whisky using complex vacuum-still technology, introduced in 1995. Grain whiskies, often despised by self-styled malt whisky aficionados, are light and sweet in character with a creamy texture and flavours of vanilla and crème anglaise.

Distillation in a patent still is a continuous process as opposed to the batch process of a malt distillery, where stills are emptied and often rested between distillations. The stills, divided into two columns (a rectifier and analyser) through which the wash is vapourised and condensed, can operate for several weeks before being closed down and cleaned. Vapours pass through copper plates in the rectifying column, delivering the same purifying effect as a pot still, and sometimes sacrificial copper is used in the spirit receiver to further enhance that process. Most of Scotland's

Single grain whisky is made from a mixture of unmalted cereals, normally maize or wheat, with a small amount of malted barley.

seven grain whisky distilleries use either Scottish and English wheat or maize, with a small proportion of malted barley to introduce the enzymes necessary for efficient fermentation. Whole grains are batch-cooked in the traditional manner, alongside some low-temperature mashing of ground wheat, supplying wort for the fermentation vessels. Fermentation takes around forty-eight hours and the wash enters the stills at around 8 per cent abv. The stills can run continuously for up to 14 days. To put the point about scale into perspective, a distillery like Cameronbridge can produce over 100 million litres of spirit a year; compare this to its recently built neighbour in Fife, the Daftmill malt whisky distillery, which has a capacity to produce just 20,000 litres a year.

FROM TENNESSEE TO TOKYO – WHISKY PRODUCTION AROUND THE WORLD

Despite bearing many similarities in the production method, Jack Daniels is not actually a bourbon. The key difference is that Jack Daniels is filtered through sugar maple charcoal prior to maturation, a process of key importance to the finished whiskey's character as a Tennessee Whiskey.

∧

Scotland's adjacent cousins in Ireland claim primacy in the history of distilling, but this is a fact disputed by those only interested in disputes. Until quite recently the only malt whiskey made in Ireland was produced at Bushmills distillery in the north, the remainder being either 'pot still' whisky or grain whisky. Traditionally Irish distillers produced whiskey from a mixture of malted and unmalted barley and sometimes other grains in gigantic pot stills, often called 'Dublin whiskey'. They also produced grain whiskey in these large pot stills. In the nineteenth century, significant amounts of this 'pot still' or 'old still' whisky was also made in Scotland at distilleries like the Caledonian in Edinburgh and Cameronbridge in Fife. 'We claim for our make superiority to the majority of the so called "Irish Whisky"', wrote John Haig & Co. of Cameronbridge in 1874, claiming their own 'Irish' whisky was 'identically the same both in material and manufacture, as "Pure Dublin Whisky'". Coffey, or patent stills, became increasingly common in the later nineteenth century, particularly in distilleries in and around Belfast. Today most Irish distilleries produce both 'pot still' and single malt whiskeys, with a number still producing grain whiskey in Coffey or patent stills. Although some distillers have experimented with peated whiskeys, the majority of Irish whiskeys are known for their lightness of flavour compared to Scotches, and their almost trademark 'smoothness', epitomised for some by the association of former England cricket captain and bon viveur David Gower (whose stylish batting was described by *Wisden Cricketers' Almanack* as 'the stuff of poetry') and the leading Irish whiskey brand, Jameson.

In North America, where the craft of distilling arrived courtesy not just of the Irish and Scots, but also continental Europeans, whiskey production took quite different paths in Canada and the United States. And so, as we will see, did its terminology, adding even more words to our already confused and overflowing whisky lexicon. Bourbon, the most famous style of whiskey from the USA, produced mostly in Kentucky, differs from Scotch production in a number of ways, although the simple conversion process that's taking place in the distillery remains the same. Each distillery has its own (nominally secret) mash bill, or combination of grains; by law it must have a minimum of 51 per cent corn, to which rye might be added for a more robust flavour, or wheat for a softer sweeter spirit. Malted barley is still required to provide the enzymes that promote the conversion process although, unlike in Scotland, the use of industrial enzymes is also permitted. Each distillery (at least by lore) also jealously guards the secret strains of yeast they use in the fermentation process, many of which were apparently hidden in limestone caves to prevent the depredations of marauding Yankees during the Civil War. Most bourbon distillers also use the sour mash process, reserving a portion of the leftovers of each still run (known as backset or stillage), which is added to every batch of mash at the start of the fermentation. The term 'sour mash' hides quite a lot of bacterial science, but its role is to ensure consistency from batch to batch. In some respects it's not dissimilar to a sourdough starter. Bourbon is sometimes double distilled in pot stills, but more often than not in the combination of a single column still, often called a beer still, and a doubler or 'thumper', which increases the purity and strength of the distillate a little like a second distillation. Sometimes a thumper might have a slobber box, a name which only demonstrates the lengths distillers will go to confuse the uninitiated. In Tennessee the Jack Daniel's and George Dickel distilleries make a type of bourbon using the Lincoln County process, where the spirit from the still is filtered through maple charcoal before being filled into casks. Hence the famous old George Dickel advertising slogan: 'as mellow as moonlight'.

In cereal-rich Canada, distilling traditions and terminologies were also inherited from European settlers although, like in the United States, the principal grain used by distillers is native corn, with the resulting spirit normally mixed with that distilled from rye in differing proportions depending on the desired outcome. As in the US, industrial enzymes may be used to promote the initial conversion process as opposed to malted barley. More recently established small distilleries, like Shelter Point on Vancouver Island, use copper pot stills imported from Scotland to distil wash from malted barley and other grains to produce malt whisky. By contrast, the larger Canadian distilleries distil with a two- or three-column distillation process, reserving pot stills for the production of so-called 'flavouring whiskies' critical in the creation of Canadian blended whisky.

Japan also owes its whisky industry to European influence, although in this case as the result of inspired industrial espionage (often, curiously, viewed through the soft-focus lenses of tartan-tinted spectacles) rather than immigration. Complacency and a colonialist arrogance led leading distillers and blenders in Scotland to disregard the presence of an inquisitive visitor from Japan armed with copious notebooks and a Brownie camera in the years immediately after the First

Suntory released their first 'Scotch Whisky' in 1929, their misappropriation of the description causing outrage in the establishment of the Scotch industry.

∧

World War. This was Masataka Taketsuru, who studied at the University of Glasgow and made himself very familiar with Scottish distilling techniques over the course of several visits to the country. He would later found the Nikka Distilling Company. When, shortly after Suntory had released their first 'Scotch Whisky' in 1929 in their home and export markets, the outraged establishment of the Scotch industry received enquiries first to allow a visit from a 'Japanese engineer' keen to tour distilleries, and then in 1930 from Thomas Cook that they might host Crown Prince Takamatsu at various distilleries. Both requests were peremptorily turned down. A belated realisation that not only had the stable door been opened, but also that the horse had definitely bolted. As a result of this much romanticised piece of piracy, Japanese distilling is still based very closely on Scottish practices and procedures. Those early visitors to Scotland had also learned the obsession that Scots blenders had with quality, something else that would be imprinted on the DNA of Japanese whisky making. With many distillers importing barley (and sometimes even peat) from the United Kingdom, and distilleries modelled closely on their Scottish counterparts, there is little to distinguish them at first sight. But the business of distilling in Japan, as we shall see, is very different from Scotland, and this has led larger distillers to build flexibility into their plant to allow them to produce different types of spirit in the same distillery, something that was rarely done in Scotland until quite recently. So you might expect to see a greater variety of still types and condensers within any single distillery than you would in Scotland. But, be that as it may, there is still little doubt that the principle objective of Japanese whisky distillers is to make the best Scotch-style whisky that they possibly can, and it cannot be denied that they have achieved some remarkable success in doing this. As it turns out, as many industry people knew but few cared to mention, some were achieving this by blending their own whiskies with bulk whisky imported from Scotland and elsewhere.

WHISKY RULES

One recent source of disquiet among whisky enthusiasts and commentators has been the fact that the rules governing the production, labelling and description of whiskies made in Japan are at best opaque (some might argue non-existent), which has led some to question the integrity of Japanese whiskies on sale around the world. However, new guidelines to be enforced from April 2024 will prohibit the longstanding practice of some Japanese distillers of blending whiskies distilled in Japan with those produced elsewhere and labelling them 'Japanese whisky'. Gainsayers complain that this inhibits innovation, while exponents say that it protects the integrity and reputation of Scotch whisky, as well as consumers. From outlawing the use of chemical additives like industrial enzymes, prohibiting tampering with casks to accelerate maturation (common in Kentucky) and forbidding the addition of flavourings (allowed in Canada), the Scotch Whisky Regulations govern every aspect of the production and marketing of Scotch. These rules are entrenched in Scottish law and are echoed in European law; for example, anything sold as 'whisky' in Europe must be at least three years old.

The rules decree that Scotch must be made in Scotland from a mash of barley and other cereals: it has to be matured in oak casks of no more than 700 litres for a minimum of three years before it can be sold as 'whisky'; an age statement on a label has to be that of the youngest whisky in the bottle and the contents of the bottle (single malt, blended Scotch whisky and so on) are properly described. Not only are the rules for Scotch tight, they are also, for the most part, quite straightforward unlike, say, in the United States, where, although there are quite strict regulations governing production of bourbon, there is no single set of rules for whiskey that approximate to the Scottish regulations. It's not just commentators and enthusiasts who rail against the regulations; commercial interests, particularly from those who wish to bring products to the market quickly, are often compromised by the

rules on maturation, minimum age and the addition of flavourings, leading some to campaign volubly against them, concealing their financial imperatives under the cloak of campaigning for freedom.

FROM TWEED TO TATTOOS

No one makes whisky without wanting to make money. This is a fact that occasionally seems lost on some enthusiasts, who despite their intrinsic mistrust of large corporations, judge other producers with a naivety that confounds any estimate of their intelligence. At the centre of this misty-eyed view of whisky making is the totemic distiller, or sometimes 'master distiller',

It's not just the image of the distillery manager that has changed over the years, but the role too. Managers are now process engineers and health and safety experts; sometimes front of house hosts, and occasionally play a key part in refining the identity and taste of a brand.

∧

a term dreamt up in the early 1990s. This slightly gruff but soft-hearted, tweed-covered father figure dispenses wisdom and good cheer (and quite possibly a few innuendo-laden quips) wherever he may travel. Like superannuated vaudevillians treading the boards for just one last farewell tour there are still a few of these stereotypes travelling the world of whisky fairs, new product launches, 'influencer' dinners and so on, with no one ever stopping to wonder who might actually be making the whisky back home. In reality the role and social position of the distillery manager has changed enormously since the 1980s, when they were still rather aloof figures overseeing a still relatively large hierarchical workforce, and were pillars of the local community. Today they are likely either to be a process engineer with a chemistry degree, or a graduate of the School of Brewing and Distilling at Edinburgh's Heriot-Watt University, which supplies certified distillers to the world. Tattoos have replaced the tweed, and piercings too (subject

Like superannuated vaudevillians treading the boards for just one last farewell tour there are still a few of these stereotypes travelling the world of whisky fairs, new product launches, 'influencer dinners' and so on, with no one ever stopping to wonder who might actually be making the whisky back home.

to health and safety regulations, of course). And while some still do trip the light fantastic across the globe, much of that brand promotional work has been taken over by highly polished and professional brand ambassadors who skit like dragonflies over the world of social media, short-lived and self-styled superstars in the shiny new world of Scotch. Distillery managers, with small multi-skilled teams of operators (generally the largest number of employees on any site will be attached to the visitor centre if there is one), spend most of their time dealing with process support, managing risk and health and safety. If they have any time left over, they are also required to host journalists, writers and important trade guests, an increasingly essential part of whisky PR. It's the operators, often these days also with diplomas in distilling from Heriot-Watt, who make the whisky. To be honest, despite the recent rise of the cult of the 'master distiller', it always has been.

THE SCIENCE OF WHISKY

There's an interesting, and long-standing tension between science and the 'practical operator', as Stuart Hastie described distillers back in the 1920s. I was once told a funny story by a friend who found himself transported from the mainland to be manager at a famous distillery on Islay. Not a week into his tenure he was awakened in the night by a call from the distillery. A crisis in the still room, could he come and help? Minutes turned into what seemed like hours as, with slide rule and notebook, calculator and pen in hand, he tried to remember something he might have been taught 30 years before as a trainee, all under the watchful eye of the long-serving and long-in-the-tooth stillman. Eventually a solution to the problem emerged, a plan of action was formulated, next steps shared. The stillman cast him a weary glance. 'Aye', he said, 'that's what we usually do when this happens.' Over decades and generations, the 'practical distillers' have developed unwritten strategies and practice from experience, not textbooks, to deal with most eventualities, as this distillery manager was gently reminded by his night-time call-out. I also recall at Clynelish a visitor asking the stillman, bent over his spirit safe, carefully measuring the strength of the distillate, when he knew how to make the cut. 'When it smells of pineapple,' he replied.

'The purely practical operator,' wrote Stuart Hastie in 1922, 'with his years-old system of trial and error has achieved much,' but he continued, 'where control from stage to stage is maintained trouble can at once be located, and, what is equally important, can frequently be located in time to allow of a remedy to be applied.' Hastie, a First World War veteran originally trained in fermentation science at William Younger's brewery in Edinburgh, had been appointed to run the newly established White Horse Distillers laboratory at Hazelburn distillery in Campbeltown after the war, quickly becoming indispensable to the company as a trouble-shooter around its distilleries and pioneering his interventionist philosophy. 'We would not be without him', wrote his boss Sir Peter Mackie in 1923, 'otherwise, we would be working by the old rule of thumb, which is no good'. By no means the first or most eminent whisky scientist – names like J A Nettleton and Philip Schidrowitz would go before him – Hastie was the most

Single malts might consistently dominate the Scotch whisky conversation, but in reality, they make up less than 10 per cent of whisky sales.

∧

I also recall at Clynelish a visitor asking the stillman, bent over his spirit safe, carefully measuring the strength of the distillate, when he knew how to make the cut. 'When it smells of pineapple,' he replied.

influential, eventually taking charge of the Distillers Company's extensive estate of malt whisky distilleries and establishing a culture of strict centralised control over processes supported by the very best science, which still exists today. The objective being, as Hastie wrote, 'increased efficiency of production resulting in possible lessened costs,' 'whisky of standardised quality and of unvarying excellence' and 'a future promise of a steadily improving spirit'. With those same objectives in mind today, with the addition of a fourth around sustainability, the craft of distilling has never been better served by scientific research carried out by individual companies such as Diageo at their Innovation and Research Centre at Menstrie near Stirling, by the industry-funded Scotch Whisky Research Institute in Edinburgh and by academic institutions all over the world.

DON'T KILL THE FISH!

One of the areas that came under Hastie's purview at Hazelburn was the issue of distilleries and pollution, which had become something of a scandal in the late nineteenth and early twentieth centuries. Albeit not the most romantic part of whisky production, the ability to dispose of effluent legally was, and remains, a critical enabler in the expansion of the distilling industry. The proliferation of new distilleries in the 1890s, particularly on Speyside, led to a series of very public legal disputes in Scotland's Court of Session between distillers and riparian owners, who claimed that the time-honoured practices of discharging pot ale or spent wash into the Spey or its tributaries, now significantly increased in volume, was damaging the fishery and livelihoods. In 1909 a Royal Commission on Sewage Disposal, which considered the matter of distillery pollution in detail, made new recommendations on permitted levels of suspended solids in effluent discharged into rivers and streams. The quest to develop new technologies to reduce the environmental impact of by-products has been going on ever since, from settling tanks to bacterial towers to biomass energy plants. At the same time, river authorities and trusts, and local and central government, introduced increasingly stringent regulations on effluent disposal – currently in Scotland the Scottish Environment Protection Agency is responsible for regulating and policing. As distilling output in Scotland increased in the 1960s and 1970s, and again in the 2010s, so did the efforts to find solutions that would enable these expansions were renewed. Sustainability is increasingly at the heart of every distiller's thinking, not least since it became apparent that investing in renewable energy not only led to a reduced use of fossil fuels and a reduction in the carbon footprints of individual sites but also delivered significant long-term savings in energy costs. And in an age where sustainability credentials are increasingly a driver of consumer choice, distillers both small and large, the world over, have embraced it as a powerful marketing point of difference. The headline '15 best eco-friendly drinks for more sustainable sipping' was ran by the *Independent* in June 2020; an abundance of press releases from distillers about new developments and new targets suggests that we are not far away from 'the world's most sustainable whisky', which will quite possibly become a new category in the still-burgeoning, and highly profitable, world of drinks' competitions.

Why is it that, try as they might, distillers find it impossible to replicate the spirit character of one distillery in another?

THE MYSTERY AND MAGIC OF WHISKY MAKING

For all the science, research and calibrations, for all the laws and regulations, for all the bamboozling terminology, there still remains an air of mystery around the art of distilling, whether practised in Scotland or anywhere else in the world. What is it that defines the unique flavour that each distillery produces? What is it that makes the product of one distillery taste so different from another located close by? And why is it that, try as they might, distillers find it impossible to replicate the spirit character of one distillery in another?

In recent years, some distillers have tried to find an explanation for this by hijacking the concept of 'terroir' from French winemakers, in an act of appropriation of the very worst kind. This concept, rich in meaning and resonance in a wine producing culture, transfers badly to whisky, as do the equally misused terms of 'vintage' and 'grand cru', perhaps unsurprisingly brought into the world of whisky by those with a background in wine. It was, for example, the St James's wine merchants Justerini & Brooks who introduced the word 'vintage' into the malt whisky lexicon when they launched Knockando single malt in the mid-1970s. The wine establishment has perennially looked down its nose at Scotch (unless they could sniff out some likely excess profits) as can still be seen quite evidently at the annual banquet and awards ceremony of the International Wine & Spirits Competition, which, while happy to receive the ever-increasing entry fees from whisky distillers anxious for a flash of gold or silver on their bottles, nonetheless treats spirits like an inconvenient afterthought. So perhaps for those from a wine background there is a sense that Scotch isn't just quite good enough, that it really needs a sprinkling of the magic dust of wine terminology to bring it up to scratch. And one might sometimes wonder if there isn't

Blended Scotch
is made by mixing
several (often many)
single malt Scotch
whiskies together
with carefully
selected single grain
Scotch whiskies.

∧

something of an inferiority complex among whisky producers themselves, which makes them yearn for a bit of the glamour and high-society *joie de vivre* of the wine trade.

But while whisky may taste of the earth, the idea that strains of barley can be equated to grape varieties and the profound impact they have on the character of wines is badly flawed. Unfortunately, this doesn't prevent the theory from attracting ardent believers, or ardent 'want-to believers'. In fact, in many different areas, the world of whisky enthusiasts is full of these people. The influence of good old John Barleycorn on spirit character, once he's been thrashed, hoaxed, ground down, boiled, boiled again, consumed and then disgorged by yeast, and then boiled again and again, before being locked, spirit broken, in the solitary confinement of an over-powering cask, is at best negligible. At very best. And as with the influence of yeast on new spirit, anything that is evident by way of specific and tangible flavour characters vanishes in the early stages of the maturation process. And there, for those newly established (or established) distilleries that can be found most vehemently proclaiming the power of terroir, is the real commercial driver of their advocacy of the concept. In the old days, distilleries made their money from selling 'fillings', newly made casks of whisky, to the large blending houses, such as Johnnie Walker or Famous Grouse. Today's new, small distilleries have no such market available to them and are reliant on selling single malts. It's a commercial imperative for them to sell as much whisky as they can, as soon as they can. But these distillers can't wait and often don't have investors with the patience to wait for ten or twelve

Terroir is less of a grand concept
and more of a cash cow.

years before they begin to turn over any money and put some cash back into the business, or the pockets of the angel investors. So they claim, their arguments echoed by compliant 'influencers', to truly understand, to truly appreciate, the influence of terroir, you have to drink the whisky young, and far younger than one would normally consider appropriate for a single malt Scotch. Terroir is less of a grand concept and more of a cash cow.

In 1907, Peter Mackie, the maverick chairman of the company who blended White Horse, owner of Lagavulin, Cragganmore and Craigellachie distilleries among others, lost the agency that his family had held for many years for the distribution of the neighbouring Laphroaig single malt whisky under acrimonious circumstances. Always impulsive, Mackie determined to build a replica of Laphroaig within the grounds of Lagavulin, employing all his local knowledge and a little skulduggery, in order to replicate the liquid he had lost the rights to. Malt Mill, as the new distillery was known, was built the following year and although it made whisky until 1962 when its buildings were incorporated within an expanded Lagavulin, it never made Laphroaig, despite Mackie's best efforts. Nor for that matter did it make Lagavulin. It made Malt Mill. Undeterred by this experience, in 1920 Mackie decided that he would change the style of whisky produced at his distillery at Hazelburn. Buoyed by his confidence in scientific knowledge and 'experiments in the laboratory' he set about making extensive changes in the distillery 'in order to eliminate the objectionable "goût" that has always been characteristic of Campbeltown whisky'. He changed the water source, employed a distiller and maltman from Speyside and used the same quality of barley employed there, claiming his spirit 'might now be taken for a North Country Glenlivet'. But the project was a failure, this hybrid Hazelburn-Kintyre whisky unsaleable. The lesson is clear: there is something at work beyond the reach of scientists and technocrats that shapes flavour, which determines character.

This is where the stolen theory of terroir gives way to the idea of place. To the idea that there is something, or some things, about a particular locale that define the character of what is made there. The place, the process, the people who mediate them. The interactions known and unknown between the three. This is where the mystery resides. When the Vienna Sausage Company in Chicago moved into a new 'state of the art' factory in the early 1970s on the Near North Side of Chicago, having deserted their original home on the Near South Side's Maxwell Street, they discovered to their horror that despite using the same meat and spice ingredients, and a replicated process, the taste and particularly texture (or 'snap') and colour of their famous Viennas was not up to scratch. A year and a half of scientific and technical enquiry could not determine the cause, or a solution. Then someone remembered an old-timer, Irving, who's job in the old plant had been to carry the sausages through a variety of rooms in the old factory, and up in an elevator to the smoke room where they were cooked. The new factory didn't have an Irving. It didn't have Irving's journey in its new continuous production line. The yet-to-be-cooked sausages in the new factory weren't subjected to the environments and changing heat levels they had formerly experienced during Irving's walk. And it turned out that this was what was missing. So they built a room where the sausages could rest before cooking, that synthesised the effect of Irving's journey. The result? The sausages got their snap back. Just like Laphroaig and Malt Mill, just like Hazelburn and its Glenlivet whisky, there was something in the place, albeit on this occasion something discoverable. It's reminiscent of the story of Clynelish whisky, which suddenly one day lost its unique trademark 'waxy' character. Scientists turned the distillery upside down trying to find out why the change had taken place without success. Then they were told that some of the intermediate vessels had been cleaned of 'gunge' prior to an inspection. Further investigation revealed that the secret of the whisky's waxiness lay in the time it spent in the spirit chargers, interacting with the accumulated 'gunge' from the low wines receiver and feints receiver, which was then passed on to the spirit stills.

Stuart Hastie, writing in the 1950s, recalled distillery managers talking to him about 'local ferments', which were, they believed, critical to determining the specific character of their single malts. Hastie, ever the scientist, did not like the idea, or the fixation that some managers had with not cleaning or disturbing certain areas of the distillery less the influence of these 'local ferments', possibly wild yeast, possibly flavour fairies, was lost. Probably the most famous of them was Roderick McKenzie at Linkwood distillery who not only insisted that the new stills fitted at the distillery in 1962 were exact replicas of the old ones, but also refused to let any cobwebs be removed from production areas and warehouses. These days no one would dare change the shape of the stills anywhere, they are carefully and patiently shaped by craftsmen in whose hands the character of the spirit partly lies. But only partly. The cobwebs may have gone, the mystery hasn't.

The lesson is clear: there is something at work beyond the reach of scientists and technocrats that shapes flavour, that determines character.

WHISKY AND WOOD

02

'No better casks for maturing whisky were ever got than the old-fashioned golden Sherry casks when second fills. Their first filling with whisky had a tendency to impart too much colour to the whisky, but as regards colour and flavour these casks, when filled with whisky for a second time, were simply splendid ensuring after say, four or five years, a whisky of very fine and useful character.'

— *Wine & Spirit Trade Record,*
  8 November 1904

THE IMPORTANCE OF WOOD

Beneath the seemingly tranquil surface of the Scotch whisky industry there exists a turmoil of rivalry and jealousy where crafts compete to be recognised as the most critical factor in determining the character and quality of the whisky. Doubtless it's the same in Ireland, or Kentucky, and Tennessee. The maltster claims they give the distiller the very best quality raw materials without which the whisky would be nothing. The coppersmith says that it's the excellence of the stills they so carefully produce, after hours of arm-wrenching hammering that guarantee quality. The distillery manager, elevated to an almost god-like status by some writers and many enthusiasts, is apparently the Svengali whose magic touch makes the whisky sing. While it's the blender who has the final say on what ends up in our glass, be it a single malt or a blended whisky, there's little doubt that in terms of creating flavours and dictating the character of the whiskies the blender has to work with, the coopers and the casks they produce are the most important. The coopers are the unsung heroes of Scotch whisky, and the story of maturation must begin with their ancient craft.

ROLL OUT THE CASKS!

Barrels, or casks as the Scotch whisky industry prefers to call them, have been used to transport and store alcoholic beverages since pre-Roman times. The strength afforded by their double arch construction is immense; the cask is intrinsically mobile and, providing the right wood is chosen, both impervious and safe for liquid storage. Scotland has a long-established wine trade with France, an aristocratic taste for imported brandy and fortified wines and had a well-developed brewing industry by the mid-eighteenth century, with small exports to Europe and North America. As such, the country was all too familiar with barrels and casks. Coopering, the construction of casks, was a thriving craft in Edinburgh, Glasgow and Aberdeen by the sixteenth century. Coopers were an important incorporated trade in each city. Barrels and casks were ubiquitous, not only for the transport and storage of wines, spirits and beer, but also water, tobacco, oil, whale blubber, paints, soap, fish, meats, butter, fruit, dried fruits, preserves, peas and pulses, sugar, tea and coffee, nails and more. Coopers and their casks were in the engine room of economic and commercial growth in the eighteenth and nineteenth centuries. To give that some sort of scale, before the First World War around a million barrels were made each year in England and Scotland just to service the herring fisheries. Coopers normally specialised in one of two disciplines, wet coopering or dry coopering, or in the United States tight or slack coopering. One for liquids, the other for everything else. Today in the United Kingdom dry coopering is considered to be an endangered craft and the small number of coopers and apprentices who still work in the trade are employed almost exclusively in the production and maintenance of casks for spirits, principally Scotch whisky. There are about 200 coopers currently working in Scotland where the trade is dominated by the French company Tonnellerie François Frères, who own four cooperages in Scotland and three in the United States. A handful

There's little doubt that in terms of creating flavours and dictating the character of whiskies, the coopers and the casks they produce are the most important. The coopers are the unsung heroes of Scotch whisky, and the story of maturation must begin with their ancient craft.

<

of distillers still retain coopers on-site; drinks giant Diageo has its own cooperage in Scotland's central belt. Around the world today coopering is focused almost exclusively on wines and spirits.

Of course the magic of the cask as far as whisky is concerned is that some woods, principally oak, not only provide a strong and safe container but also provoke a positive interaction between liquid and wood surface, leading to fundamental changes in the aroma, character and sometimes colour of the spirit. Quite when distillers, or the merchants who dealt in their goods, realised the full potential of this happy accident is unclear, although the benefits of wood maturation would have been appreciated by European winemakers and British vintners for centuries. Certainly, as distillation in Scotland grew from the first quarter of the eighteenth century, with pre-industrial distilleries in the Lowlands, and Ferintosh in the Highlands, whisky's call on the cooper would have become urgent. As the popularity of whisky grew in Scotland, though still very much a poor relation to French brandy and Jamaican rum, so grocers and wine and spirit merchants began to develop a rudimentary consumer language for Scotch whisky. This would signpost qualitative differences in whiskies to potential buyers, and at the same time flatter their knowledge or nascent connoisseurship. From the 1750s it became increasingly common for advertisers to stress the provenance of their whiskies, from the Highlands, from the North Country, or very specifically from the famous Ferintosh. This celebrated whisky, from an estate on the Black Isle, north of Inverness, had won an exemption from the payment of duties on spirit distilled from the estate's own barley as compensation for damage done to the distillery by Jacobites in 1689. The exemption was lost in 1784, leading the poet Robert Burns to lament in verse 'Thee, Ferintosh! O sadly lost!' In the last quarter of the century, age – time spent in the wood – also began to be used as a signifier of quality and used as a rationale for price differentiation. In 1781, the Ferintosh Company's shop in Edinburgh was selling 'spirits of a proper age, and well flavoured';

nine years later James Watson, also in Edinburgh began to sell 'genuine' two-year-old malt whisky that he deemed equal to any rum for making punch. In 1793, John Ker in Edinburgh advertised five grades of whisky, each one more expensive than the other: 'malt whisky', 'fine malt whisky', 'very fine malt whisky', 'one year old superfine whisky' and 'two years old superfine whisky'. With a shameless use of hyperbole that would not be out of place in some of today's promotional materials, Ker's advert might well be considered to be the birth of whisky marketing. It certainly helped to put age and maturation firmly on the whisky map. In the new century, when George IV visited Edinburgh, Elizabeth Grant recalled in her memoirs that she was instructed by her father to find 'whisky long in the wood' to present as a gift to the sovereign. A couple of years later, an early guide to mixing whiskies urged blenders 'to be careful in purchasing spirits from the distiller as old as possible'. Age, the influence on flavour of that time spent 'in the wood', had become one of the defining measures of the quality of Scotch.

BARRELS, BUTTS AND HOGSHEADS ...

Before moving on to talk about the process of maturation, it's probably timely to say something about casks, or barrels as they are called in the United States and Canada. At Diageo's Cambus Cooperage in Clackmannanshire casks are stored in a barrel park. A cask is made up of wooden staves, which when softened by steam are raised into a double-arch structure, secured by metal hoops of varying circumferences. Each end of the cask has a wooden cask head, and in the centre of the cask body there will be a bung, through which the cask can be filled, or emptied. Whether built purely by the cooper's hand, or with the assistance of machinery in an automated cooperage, whisky casks feature no nails or fixatives like glue; metal hoops, driven by hand or machinery, hold the structure together. The size of casks can vary.

In Scotland the most common are American standard barrels (190 litres), hogsheads (250 litres), butts (500 litres) and puncheons (550 litres). Occasionally distillers may use smaller casks, often in an attempt to speed up the maturation process, such as quarter-casks (50 litres), or casks more commonly associated with certain wines, such as port-pipes (500 litres). Casks weren't only used for maturing newly made malt or grain whisky; up until the 1960s and 1970s puncheons were used for storing blends before bottling, and casks in diminishing quantities for bulk sales of blends, which were probably on a par with bottled sales in the nineteenth century. In Scotland, once filled, casks are stored in bonded warehouses; warehouses, or bonds, come in various shapes and sizes. Dunnage warehouses, found at older distilleries, are normally stone built, with thick walls, occasional barred windows and earth or ash floors. Casks are stacked three high in what are called 'stows'. Some, like the warehouse at Lagavulin, which faces out to sea, have had additional floors added over time. At its Blackgrange site in Clackmannanshire, Diageo has around four million casks of maturing Scotch whisky stored in around 60 concrete warehouses, many stained black by the whisky fungus, *Baudoinia compniacensis*, which frequently occurs at distilleries and maturation sites around the world. This fungus is, at the time of writing, at the centre of class action cases being heard in courts in Scotland and the United States, brought on behalf of property owners who claim their formerly pristine new homes have been despoiled by its inexorable spread. Though it must be said, it's a bit like building a house next to a church and then complaining about the bell ringing every Sunday.

So, what is it that happens when whisky goes into a cask that makes it so different and apparently so much better? In short, it's the interaction between the spirit and the wood; the wood taking away unwanted flavour elements from the spirit and then giving a range of desirable flavours, in processes called subtractive and additive maturation. But very few woods deliver the type of maturation that distillers and blenders require for their spirit. Two varieties of oak, American white oak and European oak, provide the casks used not only in Scotland, but in the overwhelming majority of distilling countries. Recently Japanese or mizunara oak has been used in the maturation of Japanese, American, Scotch and Irish whiskies. Other woods such as chestnut have been used in the past for whisky maturation, although in 1929 the Whisky Association, the forerunner of today's Scotch Whisky Association, issued the first classification of casks used in the whisky trade that outlawed its use. Having said that, the exigencies created by the two world wars did sometimes lead distillers to make use of other materials when shortages arose. The properties of American and European oak that delight the cooper are strength and durability, and at the same time workability, particularly when it comes to shaping staves, the individual components of the cask's body. The structure of these oaks is also impervious, so well-made casks won't leak, and porous, which allows air into the casks, enabling the spirit to 'breathe'. For the distiller and blender an additional bonus is that an oak cask, particularly once its staves have been charred or toasted, will not only extract unwanted (often sulphury) elements from the new spirit, but will release a variety of compounds, particularly vanillins and tannins, lactones and hemicellulose, which add flavour and colour. When a cask is charred, the internal surface of the staves are ignited by a flame for a short period of minutes before being extinguished; when they are toasted, a flame is still used but the surface does not ignite. Traditionally casks in Scotland are toasted while barrels in the United States are charred.

American standard barrels or ASBs (190 litres), hogsheads (250 litres) and butts (500 litres) are among the most common casks used for maturing Scotch and other whiskies.

OLD CASKS FOR NEW

These flavours are far more intense when new casks are first used for maturing whisky. Until the Second World War, distillers in Scotland used a mixture of what was called new, or plain wood, coopered in Scotland from imported American oak staves from the United States, Canada and sometimes the Baltic, and casks that had previously held wines such as sherry (which we'll talk about shortly, see page 57) and Madeira, or spirits such as brandy and rum. These new, or plain, casks would have made up the majority of those in use, although today it's quite exceptional for new wood to be used in Scotland, and when it is it's often somewhat ironically described as an 'innovation', despite the commonality of its use in the past. However, using new wood is still the practice of many American distillers, particularly in Kentucky and Tennessee, and it is the distinctive sweetness and flavour of vanilla that is one of the trademark signatures of bourbon whiskeys. Cooperages in Kentucky produce new barrels to very exacting, and secret, specifications from their individual customers, particularly when it comes to charring and toasting, where the depth of the char can determine what specific outcomes the barrels will deliver. An intense, or heavy, charring might also mean that the desired level of maturation can be achieved more quickly, one of the holy grails of whisky makers the world over. There is no minimum age for whiskeys to be bottled and consumed in the United States, unlike Europe where, as we have seen, whisky must be at least three years old. However to be called a 'straight' whiskey, like Jim Beam or Woodford Reserve, the whiskey must have been matured, by federal law, for a minimum of two years in charred oak barrels.

Very often these whiskeys are four, six, or eight years old before they are bottled. But at that point the barrel's life for maturing bourbon has come to an end. Tradition has it that American distillers only used barrels once because wood was relatively cheap and whiskey barrels could easily be usefully repurposed, and because they came to recognise that the intense flavours they demanded were diminished if barrels were reused. Whether true or not, in 1935 in order to offer some protection to the newly re-established cooperage industry in the wake of both Prohibition and the Great Depression, federal laws were changed to decree that only new charred oak barrels could be used for the maturation of bourbon. Scottish distillers had experimented using American whiskey casks for maturation at the start of Prohibition, when significant quantities of American whiskeys were dumped on to the UK market, but found them largely unsatisfactory due to the heavy charring. In the years after the Second World War, however, with wood for new casks in short supply and production levels rising, distillers turned to America again, importing increasing quantities of these once-used ex-bourbon casks. Readily available, they were first imported as complete barrels, but later broken down in the USA into shooks, or bundles of staves, and rebuilt at cooperages in Scotland often as larger hogsheads. The wood surface of these ex-bourbon casks is still active, so they are normally first used in Scotland for grain whisky maturation, where strong vanillin characters are considered desirable. The use of newly coopered wood in the 1970s and 1980s became increasingly rare and today over 80 per cent of all the scotch whisky maturing in Scotland is held in ex-bourbon casks of one sort or another.

An intense, or heavy, charring might also mean that the desired level of maturation can be achieved more quickly, one of the holy grails of whisky makers the world over.

THE MATHEMATICS OF MATURATION

Time is a key element in the maturation process, but location, temperature, the size of the cask and the number of times it has been used, or 'filled', are all a vital part of the tale too. The maturation processes are sequential. First the subtractive, then the additive and finally the 'interactive' phase. Different styles of whisky mature at different rates, the heavier more old-fashioned 'meaty' styles normally needing more time in the wood than the lighter. The size of the cask, the amount of wood surface area that is available to the spirit to interact with will also determine the speed of the process, as will the 'activity' of the wood surface. Distillers love to reuse casks if they are able to. As casks are filled, disgorged or emptied, and then refilled, so the wood surface exposed to the sprit will become 'exhausted', or 'inactive'. A little used or 'active' wood surface will provide a more intense maturation than an 'inactive' one. The previous contents of the cask will also affect the results of maturation, not because there may be some wine or whisky left slopping around the cask when it is newly filled, but because the previous contents will have interacted with the exposed wood surface and changed its make-up, in a way that will then affect the types of compounds that influence flavours and colours in subsequent maturations. This influence, no doubt originally learned by a process of trial and error, can be profound.

In Scotland, whiskies normally mature at a pretty constant temperature all year round and anyone familiar with Scotland's climate will understand this to be 'cold'. It's a slow, even process; ideal, the more patient would say, for producing great whisky. Winter temperatures in Kentucky are at or around freezing, in the summer they can be in excess of 30°C. In older-style warehouses or rickhouses there, some walled with corrugated iron, the whiskeys almost cook in July and August when the internal temperatures at the top of the warehouses can be over

40°C. Until very recently Kentucky distillers used to move casks around the warehouses to even out the effect of these temperature variations in order to ensure consistency in the final whiskey. Today, the Buffalo Trace distillery in Kentucky has an experimental 'Warehouse X' dedicated to researching the effect of climate on maturation, including a section with no roof. Heat not only accelerates maturation but also increases the amount of spirit that is lost through evaporation, a result of the porosity of the barrels. This phenomenon is now commonly known as 'the angels' share', a phrase of uncertain origin apparently borrowed by the Scots from French cognac producers in the 1970s. In Scotland a 2 per cent loss per year is allowed: in Kentucky the annual rate can be as high as 6 per cent. In 2012 veteran whisky writer Charlie MacLean appeared in a Ken Loach film, *The Angels' Share*, about the sale of a mythical cask of whisky. Charlie played whisky expert Rory McAllister, a barely disguised pastiche of himself.

Some will argue that the very specific location of a warehouse will have an effect on the way a whisky matures in the cask, an extension of the flawed terroir argument (see page 19), which plays well into the hands of small distillers with minimal warehousing requirements. Many larger distilleries in Scotland long outgrew the capacity of their original warehouses, and not all have either access to land, or the desire to blight rural landscapes with large modern industrial storage complexes. Larger companies with multiple distilleries began developing new 'out of town' centralised warehousing complexes in the 1960s as post-war production soared, a process given a greater sense of urgency following the Cheapside Fire in Glasgow in March 1960, when a blaze at a whisky warehouse in a cramped part of the city led to the death of 19 fire officers after a wall collapsed as casks exploded. Today some of these firms, like Diageo with its 27 malt whisky distilleries, tanker new make spirit to centralised fillin stores and then on to one of several massive warehouse facilities. For the wistful romantics this severs an umbilical cord between the spirit and its place of birth, and some say, compromises both the quality and integrity of the whiskies concerned.

On the other hand, there's no evidence that the location of maturation impacts on the character or quality of individual Scotch whiskies. Scotland is a small country with a pretty consistent maritime climate; whiskies will mature at the same rate on the west or east coast, or the central belt. It's nice to think that your whisky might have rested for years in an old cobweb-filled dunnage warehouse with saltwater and seaweed crashing against the stone walls during wild Hebridean storms, but the reality is that the size and scale of the industry rarely allows for that. And as for the saltwater and seaweed influencing a whisky's flavour, an idea much loved by advertising copywriters in the 1980s (and remarkably sometimes today) – well, that takes the idea of terroir into the realms of pure fantasy.

It's nice to think that your whisky might have rested for years in an old cobweb-filled dunnage warehouse with saltwater and seaweed crashing against the stone walls during wild Hebridean storms, but the reality is that the size and scale of the industry rarely allows for that.

THE LORD LIEUTENANT'S WHISKY

One of the elements of Scotch whisky maturation that seems to most fascinate enthusiasts is the use of sherry casks, about which much is written, but little fully understood. Sherry consumption in the United Kingdom grew rapidly after the liberalisation of the wine trade by Gladstone as Chancellor of the Exchequer in 1860. Sherry also benefitted in terms of popularity from the endorsement of the highly influential medical profession. In 1873 the British public consumed over six million gallons of sherry, but by 1900 this figure had slumped to a mere one and a half million. It seemed sherry was seriously falling out of favour. This was largely due to issues of declining quality as greedy producers compromised on standards in order to take advantage of the boom, as a result of which the medical lobby withdrew their support for the wine in favour of the new fashionable drink, blended Scotch whisky. Sherry was shipped to England, Ireland and Scotland in butts and bonded, sometimes for many years, in large warehouses in ports like London, Bristol, Dublin and Leith. Once emptied, the casks were surplus to the requirements of the wine merchant. Primacy in the use of these unwanted sherry casks was given not to the Scots but to Irish distillers, and particularly to Kinahan's of Dublin, whose LL whiskey was one of the leading Irish brands. As a consequence, wrote a nineteenth-century trade journal, Irish whiskey 'became by custom a coloured spirit, whereas Scotch was supposed to be white, and in the great majority of cases was so sold'. In a counterfeit case in 1863 the firm claimed that the founder had, around the turn of the century, 'originated and adopted a method of preparing whiskey whereby the quality was improved and a peculiar flavour imparted to the whiskey', the secret of which was not revealed in court. By the 1840s, Kinahan's LL whiskey, was being advertised in England as being 'stored in sherry butts'. The Scots, argued the trade journal, adopted the process having seen how popular Irish whiskeys had become in the first half of the nineteenth century, adding that 'we are not sure that the taste for the Scotch article has not been largely due to the softness and roundness imparted by maturing the article in fresh sherry wood'. It was quite clear that the addition of colour from sherry casks helped too and would very much change the appearance of Scotch in the future; today drinkers would baulk at the thought of mature Scotch ever being an almost clear spirit. A handbook on Scotch whisky written in 1825 observed, almost with surprise, 'that there are a great many people fonder of a dram that has received a tinge than that which is clear and transparent'.

The sherry casks that Scotch distillers and blenders were most interested in were the freshly emptied butts that had been bonded prior to use. At the height of the sherry trade, these were sometimes being returned to Spain as demand from distillers wasn't sufficient to use them. However, whisky production increased almost threefold during the period that sherry consumption declined by around 75 per cent. Added to which, by the late nineteenth century, major shippers of sherry brands were beginning to export in bottles, not wood. The result was a dramatic decline in the availability of freshly emptied butts and an equally dramatic rise in their price, from around twelve shillings in 1860 to close to fifty shillings in 1900. There was also, argued some, an equal decline in the quality of many of the butts available, and constant grumbling that the trade was victim of 'a swindle', many of the so-called 'freshly emptied' casks having hardly held sherry for more than a few months. The decline in demand for sherry meant that some producers in Spain could ship bodega butts used in sherry production for sale, but their availability was finite. Distillers looked to alternatives, and both Marsala and Madeira began to be shipped in butts to meet their needs. Other sherry markets around the world, principally in Europe and the United States, were scoured for butts, although their suitability for use often suffered due to

Two varieties of oak, American white oak and European oak, provide the casks used not only in Scotland, but in the overwhelming majority of whisky making countries.

∨

poorer quality wines and the ravages of shipping. One estimate was that by the turn of the century the supply of freshly emptied casks was only sufficient to fill around 3 per cent of the whisky being produced in Scotland. Spain also began producing wine-seasoned hogsheads crafted from American oak, which were filled briefly with wine (often of a variable quality) before being shipped to Glasgow or Leith for the use of Scottish distillers. This idea of wine-seasoned casks was also adopted in Scotland, most notably by W P Lowrie of Glasgow, who in addition to coopering had an extensive bonding and blending business. In 1888, Lowrie patented a method for seasoning casks prior to filling using steam-injection to open up the pores of the wood. The addition of wine to the process produced, he argued, a far higher quality of cask than the seasoned casks coming from Spain. Sherry shippers Williams and Humbert argued that the most economical and effective answer to the shortage rested in American oak hogsheads that had been scalded and filled with Pedro Ximénez, a dark, rich and intensely sweet sherry, for a fortnight prior to use; by 1907 they were advertising paxarette blending sherry 'used by all the leading Whisky Blenders in Scotland, Ireland and the USA'. Paxarette was a seasoning syrup based on Pedro Ximénez. Others advocated the use of additives, such as prune wine, as a cost-saving shortcut.

As more sherry shippers chose to export their brands in bottles during the first half of the twentieth century, freshly emptied bonded butts that had been so highly prized became increasingly scarce, save from large sherry houses such as Harveys of Bristol. As we've mentioned before, wood shortages and import difficulties caused by two world wars also exacerbated supply difficulties. While wine-seasoned casks and small numbers of bodega casks (made from both American and European oak) were still sourced directly from Spain, paxarette-treated casks became the standard in the industry in place of 'sherry casks'. Treatment varied from pressurised systems similar to that patented by Lowrie, to simply painting the insides of new or emptied casks and sometimes blending vats with paxarette. Under revised Scotch whisky regulations introduced in 1990 the use of paxarette was outlawed, so those in search of 'sherry casks' either had to source them (mostly wine-seasoned) from Spain, or, like Diageo, produce them in Scotland at their own 'bodega'. Although today's sherried whiskies are a far cry from those of the nineteenth century, they are still highly prized by enthusiasts as single malts, and judicious use of them in blends as a 'top dressing' is often the equivalent of the blender's icing on the cake. These whiskies are often rich in colour (think shades of mahogany) with a sweet wine character, full of rich fruits and sometimes chocolate, with a drying finish. 'Sherry bombs' for which some distilleries are famous, can be the most sublime examples of this style of whisky. But be warned: 'overcooked' sherried whiskies can sometimes be overwhelming in their character, displaying rubbery or sometimes sulphury aromas and flavours. Despite their apparent sweetness they can also be mouth-puckeringly dry, masking any evidence of the effort the distiller made to produce their prized distillery character.

'Sherry bombs' for which some distilleries are famous, can be the most sublime examples of this style of whisky.

WOODMAN, WOODMAN, SPARE THAT TREE!

It takes an American or European oak 80–100 years to reach maturity and be suitable to be made into a cask. The cost of casks is a huge investment for distillers, and they naturally want to make the most of these precious assets. So it's no surprise that casks are reused by distillers the world over, except in those whiskey-producing areas of the United States where it is mandatory to use new oak. Each time a cask is used, the wood surface becomes less active until it is, as distillers say, exhausted. Some distillers use a tintometer to measure the colour of the whisky each time a cask is emptied – the colour level will diminish each time until 'exhaustion' is reached. A cask might be used, or filled, four or five times before it's exhausted. Every fill has to last a minimum of three years for Scotch whisky, but it could be eight, ten, twelve or more. And remember, most ex-bourbon casks will be between four and eight years old before they receive their 'first fill' of Scotch or other whisky. So a cask might easily be forty or fifty years old before it reaches exhaustion. Once destined only for garden centres or barbecues, recent developments in applied wood-science have led to the development and widespread adoption of the process of cask rejuvenation. Coopers used to try to extend the life of a cask by cleaning the inside with heavy wire brushes and then charring the exposed surface. Today, exhausted casks are sent back to the cooperage, the inside of the cask staves shaved and re-toasted to exacting specifications in order to reactivate the wood and give the cask a new lease of life. It is quite possible that casks can go through at least two of these rejuvenations before the integrity of the cask structure is compromised, meaning that the life of an active cask could extend well beyond the time it takes an oak to reach maturity, something of a triumph for sustainability.

When Stuart Hastie began his work at the Hazelburn laboratory in the early twentieth century, distillers, although troubled by the cost and availability of certain kinds of casks, did not appear to think that learnings from science could be applied to wood. They certainly didn't have phrases such as 'wood science' and 'wood technology'. Yet this has been one of the most intensive areas of scientific research into whisky in recent years. Experiments have been conducted into the use of different varieties of oak and other woods, including the once outlawed chestnut, to assess their suitability for maturation and their ability to deliver novel flavours, or simply eye-catching marketing stories, particularly for start-ups desperate to have their voice heard in a noisy marketplace. It might be eyebrow raising that Chivas Regal Mizunara, a blended Scotch whisky, some of which has been matured in Japanese mizunara oak, commands a price premium of over 100 per cent compared with the similarly aged Chivas Regal 12 Year Old, but it's a perfect example of how applied wood science can not only drive innovation, but also profitability. Patents have been taken out for hexagonal casks, both easier to store but also providing a greater wood surface to promote faster maturation; square casks have been used for secondary 'finishing'. The effects of microwaves on wood structure and maturation processes have also been examined in depth. Oak inserts have been placed in casks in an attempt to increase the apparent maturity of

A cask might easily be
40 or 50 years old before
it reaches exhaustion

younger whiskies, a practice outlawed in Scotland but still permitted in Kentucky. In the United States, at least one distiller plays loud east-coast hip-hop through a warehouse in the belief that sound waves can accelerate flavour development. Some years ago, Diageo began experimenting with shrink-wrapped casks in an attempt to prevent the angels from getting their due share of the distiller's work. When news of the experiment was leaked in the Scottish press, critics argued that preventing the casks from breathing would not only finish off the angels, but would also taint the maturation process. The results of the trials are unknown, but for a company with over ten million maturing casks, depriving the angels could save the equivalent of the output of a large, modern distillery, such as Roseisle on Speyside, annually.

In the United States, at least one distiller broadcasts loud east-coast hip-hop through a warehouse in the belief that sound waves can accelerate ageing and flavour development.

TWO CASKS ARE BETTER THAN ONE?

Nowhere has the impact of wood research and understanding on consumer choice been more evident than in the field of wood finishing. This process was pioneered commercially in Scotch whisky by William Grant with their Balvenie Classic (now Balvenie DoubleWood) in the 1990s, and is now a method used by distillers and blenders all over the world. The process, which involves the transfer of whisky from its original cask to another with characteristics that might either improve or alter its flavour, is in reality a long-established practice in the wine and spirits trade known as 're-racking'. While re-racking was a permitted yet undeclared activity carried out discretely behind warehouse or cellar doors, Balvenie brought 'finished' whiskies to fans and drinkers in a range of innovations starting with DoubleWood, and then their PortWood finish a few years later. They were followed in what would become a rush of lookalike innovations by Glenmorangie, who launched a PortWood Finish in 1994, and United Distillers (now Diageo), who released sherry- and port-wood finishes of their Classic Malts range in 1997. Pandora's box had been opened and finishing became ubiquitous.

The normal process for producing a finished whisky is that a series of casks from a particular distillery will be disgorged and re-racked into casks, which have typically previously held wines or fortified wines, although the use of spirit casks such as rum is not unknown. The finishing casks may have held their first liquid as part of a normal production process, or they may have been specially prepared to deliver a very rapid result, and treated or seasoned with the wine in question. For a 'one-distillery, one-brand' company like Glenmorangie, cask finishing released them from the straitjacket of age-statement led innovations; after all, there is a limit to the number of those you can reasonably produce. Finishing allowed them to build a formidable on-shelf

The process of wood finishing was pioneered commercially in Scotland by William Grant & Sons in the 1990s. Balvenie brought 'finished' whiskies to fans and drinkers in a range of innovations starting with DoubleWood, and then their PortWood finish a few years later.

∧

presence around the world, and, of course, exotic-sounding finished whiskies with enhanced packaging and impenetrable code numbers command a higher price than regular bottlings. While the majority of early releases carried age statements, finishing soon began to be seen by some as a way of adding character to younger whiskies through an intense, short, sharp shock of a second maturation, bringing them to the market earlier and more profitably than might have been possible. Many whisky enthusiasts have tired of the endless stream of sometimes unlikely finishes, which now range from beer casks (Diageo released, perhaps inadvisably, a Guinness cask-finished expression of Lagavulin) to, rather mischievously, an unofficial herring cask finish ('fishky') of Bruichladdich. Some have criticised brands for trying to trade on the reputation of the producers whose casks they have used for finishing, others have argued that finishing diminishes the singularity and distinctiveness of the single malt Scotch whisky category by blurring the flavour parameters normally associated with Scotch. Others see it as a boon to innovation, bringing new drinkers into the world of whisky. Critics have maintained that the quality of some of the new products released in the 2000s was simply not up to scratch. The Scotch Whisky Association, somewhat after the event, have tried to restrain some of the more unlikely combinations by initially appealing to 'traditional practice', although it's unclear who might be the final arbiter of determining this. Recent changes to the regulations, for example, have permitted the use of tequila casks for secondary maturation, but not casks that have been used to age stone fruit liquids or cider. For the record, and thinking of what might define a 'traditional practice', the first reference to tequila being drunk in the United Kingdom seems to come from 1925 when it was being served at The Savoy in London by Harry Craddock, the hotel's famous American barman. On the other side of the Atlantic, distillers have even used Tabasco casks to mature their whiskey.

two hundred years, particularly in Scotland, and if we agree with the experts that something like 70 per cent of the flavour of whisky is governed by the wood, there is little doubt that today's whiskies must be very different from those of a hundred years ago, let alone two hundred. That's certainly not to suggest that today's whiskies are inferior. A minimum age for the maturation of Scotch of three years was only introduced during the First World War; prior to that blended 'tap whisky', sold in pubs and bars, might have only been a year old, if that. Age statements were rare, there were a few leading brands like Johnnie Walker Black Label that carried a 12-year age statement from 1906, although when the ravages of war depleted aged stocks this became something of an albatross around the necks of its makers. Many believed that whisky was at its best at around ten years old and it was thought that after the age of fifteen years it developed positively unpleasant 'slimy' characteristics.

Today, when standard blends of Scotch without age statements are probably between six and eight years old, both single malts and blended Scotches carry age statements far in excess of this. While

Many believed that whisky was at its best at around ten years old and it was thought that after the age of 15 years it developed positively unpleasant 'slimy' characteristics.

often not as outstanding as the age, price and publicity might seduce people into believing, the very old whiskies can sometimes be quite remarkable. And let's not forget, lest there be any doubt, that when you see an age statement on a bottle of Scotch it always refers to the youngest whisky in the bottle. Before Lloyd George's famous budget of 1909, which dramatically increased the duty on spirits, and the First World War, most Scotch whiskies were drunk at proof, or ten under proof, that is to say around 51–57 per cent abv.. Today the minimum strength for Scotch whisky is 40 per cent abv and the majority of Scotches, both blends and single malts, are bottled at between 41–43 per cent. In the 1920s, some distillers and blenders sought to return to 'pre-war strength' as some early whisky experts lamented the loss of character that the reduction had caused, but consumers and the economics of the industry dictated that the lower strength became the norm.

Over the past ten years or so, new entrants to distilling, not just in Scotland, but all over the world, have sought to subvert the traditional narratives around the importance of 'time in the wood' in order to get quicker returns from what is often an unfeasibly long-term investment. Distilling lighter styles of spirit that will mature more quickly in active ex-bourbon casks delivers a product to market in three, rather than eight, ten or twelve years, albeit without the complexity that 'time in the wood' gives. They are also subverting traditional narratives around age and price. As we saw at the beginning of this chapter, as early as 1903 writers were mourning the passing of the golden age of the freshly emptied sherry cask. Whiskies were, wrote another, 'less sweet, lighter and dryer'. That was a hundred years ago and since then bourbon casks and seasoned 'sherry casks' (and for a while paxarette) have become the norm in maturation. So, today's whiskies are undoubtedly different from the past. They continue to evolve, reflecting the reality of whisky making today; from commercial imperatives to changing consumer tastes and even, as we shall see later, changes in the way that whisky is drunk.

WHISKY AND FREEDOM

03

'Good whisky-punch, well made,
is certainly of all the tipples ever
invented by mortal man, the most
insinuating and the most loving,
because, more than any other, it
disposes the tippler to be pleased
with himself. It brightens his hopes,
assuages his sorrows, crumbles down
his difficulties, softens the hostility
of his enemies, and, in fact, inclines
him, for the time being, to think
generously of all mankind … '

— *Hampshire Telegraph*, 4 April 1832

'FREEDOM AN' WHISKY
GANG THEGITHER'

Few can have done more to establish the reputation of Scotch
as Scotland's national drink than the whisky-punch-loving poet
Robert Burns. His eulogies to whisky reflected both his strong
sense of patriotism and his belief in individual liberty; for Burns,
Scotch was an egalitarian drink, *the people's drink*. Important
though this sentiment was, it was to be whisky blending that truly
democratised Scotch whisky in the second half of the nineteenth
century. It was because of blending that Scotch became, as a
result of the accessibility of both the taste and price that blending
afforded it, Scotland's gift to the world. Today blends like Johnnie
Walker, Chivas Regal, Dewar's and Buchanan's straddle the globe,
as do famous blends of whisky from Canada, Ireland and Japan.
While they can seem quite ordinary in their home market, Scotch
whisky blends like Johnnie Walker Red Label are highly prized in
overseas markets, aspirational luxuries for those with their feet
on the first rungs of the ladder of prosperity and social success.
As we have seen, blended Scotch whisky accounts for around
90 per cent of all the Scotch that's sold in the world, and is as
firmly established in the vibrant drinking cultures in countries like
Sweden, France, the United States, Russia and South Africa as it
is in Scotland. With over 90 per cent of the whisky that's made in
Scotland being exported, it's clear that, despite Burns's patriotism
about this so-called 'national drink', Scotch has become the
world's drink. Although it bears mentioning that if you ask a Scot,
'what's your poison?' they're more likely to choose a cold glass of
vodka over whisky. That being said, whisky was encouraging the
world to sing, in perfect harmony or otherwise, generations before
soft drinks like Coca-Cola.

WHO INVENTED WHISKY?

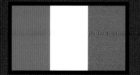

IRELAND

SCOTLAND

NOT FOR ALL THE TEA IN CHINA ...

Brand owners and their clever marketeers often like to imply that the founders of their blended Scotch brands somehow invented or 'pioneered' the blending process. The truth is that families like the Walkers of Kilmarnock, the Ushers of Edinburgh, the Dewars of Perth or the Greenlees brothers from Campbeltown were simply better at it, more determined and more successful than those thousands of other businesses that were blending Scotch in Scotland, and England, in the nineteenth century. No one 'invented' blending. It was second nature to grocers and wine and spirit merchants to mix things together – indeed it was one of the essential skills of their trade. The huge growth in the consumption of tea in the late eighteenth century encouraged grocers to blend both different qualities of the same varieties of tea, and also to blend varieties together. They soon learned, or were taught, that some teas in relatively small quantities could have a profound and positive effect on larger quantities of others: 'one ounce of Pekoe in a pound of fine Souchong' advised *The Tea Purchaser's Guide* in 1785, 'gives an excellent flavour'. As it was to turn out, the same could be said of blending whiskies. Blending smaller quantities of powerful Highland whiskies with lighter lowland malts or grain whiskies also happened to give 'an excellent flavour'.

Beyond flavour, the careful blending of tea also gave the grocer opportunities for increased profits; broadly speaking the more flavoursome the tea, the more expensive it became. There was, however, one shadow that hung over blended tea, and that was the suspicion of adulteration. It was not unusual for teas to arrive from China that had been cut with other similar organic materials, such as fatsi leaves, but some argued that the practice went on in the home market too, others promoted the idea that simply mixing one tea varietal with another was a form of deceit. During the nineteenth century the suspicion that blending was somehow an underhand way to defraud consumers became widespread, and

The Irish and Scotch whisky industries have a long-standing history of battling against one another. Blended Scotch is often described as 'Scotland's gift to the world' but the origins of the first distilled whisky remain hotly disputed by some.

<

was validated by very public scandals around the adulteration of a variety of foodstuffs, notably milk and margarine, bulked up with sometimes dangerous additives. This mistrust of blending would have serious consequences for blended Scotch whisky.

IT'S ALL IN THE MIX!

The mixing of whiskies from a number of distilleries to produce a vatting or blend for sale was certainly commonplace by the start of the nineteenth century. A guide for grocers and innkeepers published in 1825 advised on how blends might be put together: 'if both the malt and grain whisky is good two thirds of the grain whisky may be added to one third of malt whisky, or two gallons of grain and one of malt whisky, without the mixture being known by those who consider themselves judges'. The whisky, it urged, should be bought 'as old as possible' and giving the blend additional time to develop (or 'marrying' as the industry calls it today) was strongly recommended. The author also suggested adding beer to the blend to give body, flavour and colour, one of many past practices that are now outlawed

If both the malt and grain whisky is good two thirds of the grain whisky may be added to one third of malt whisky, or two gallons of grain and one of malt whisky, without the mixture being known by those who consider themselves judges.

under the Scotch Whisky Regulations. Surviving inventories would suggest that early blends were made from a relatively small number of individual whiskies, often chosen from distilleries that were easily accessible. The whiskies that John Walker used in his early blends were principally from Islay, Campbeltown and the central belt; blenders in Edinburgh, Perth or Aberdeen were also most likely to use locally produced whiskies resulting in the development of 'regional' styles of blends – the smokier from the west, rich and fruity from the east – flavours which still survive to an extent today. The opening up of the Highlands by the newly built railways in the middle of the nineteenth century dramatically increased the availability of single malt whiskies to blenders, but it was changes in the excise laws that really kickstarted blending of the style and scale that we might recognise today.

Between 1853–64 a series of changes in the excise laws allowed first the mixing of malt whisky in bonded premises, then the blending of malt and grain whiskies under bond for sale in the home market and, finally, for sale in export. In addition, the duties paid on spirits in England and Scotland were equalised in 1855, bringing an end to cross-border smuggling and opening the critical English market to Scottish distillers and blenders. It is often claimed that Andrew Usher & Co. of Edinburgh, famous for their brand Old Vatted Glenlivet, were the first company to take advantage of these changes, and therefore deserving of the title of 'the first blenders'. James Dunlop, a Leith shipping agent, received a dispensation from the Board of Customs as early as 1851, two years before the laws were first changed, to vat or mix malt whisky in bond for sale in Ship's Stores and for general export. His brand was 'a vat of the finest Scotch Highland Whiskies, comprising Glenlivet, Balmoral, Islay, Campbeltown and Lochnagar'. The brand would

The huge growth in the consumption of tea in the late eighteenth century encouraged grocers to blend both different qualities of the same varieties of tea, and also to blend different varieties together. They soon learned that some teas in relatively small quantities could have a profound and positive effect on larger quantities of others. As it was to turn out, the same was true of blending whiskies.

later pass to the Leith firm Robertson, Sanderson & Co., who claimed it as the 'oldest whisky trademark in Scotland'. Dunlop had prepared several thousand gallons of Mountain Dew (not to be confused with the modern fizzy drink) bottled and 'packed in Scottish heather'. All that was needed was that final change to allow malt and grain whisky to be blended together under bond and the modern business of blending Scotch whisky had been born.

Mid-nineteenth-century malt whisky, particularly of the heavily flavoured sort from Campbeltown or Islay, was never going to be a drink that would capture the imagination or taste of the growing middle classes in England, particularly London, the place where reputations were made, and a shop window to the world. It was these lighter styles of blended whisky, still with an abundance of character for these new whisky drinkers, and with names and labels redolent of the wild and romantic Highlands and highlanders so much loved by Queen Victoria, that almost certainly would.

While deplored by traditionalists and malt distillers in the Highlands, grain whisky was the critical element that cemented the success of Scotch blends. Mid-nineteenth-century malt whisky, particularly of the heavily flavoured sort from Campbeltown or Islay, was never going to be a drink that would capture the imagination or taste of the growing middle classes in England, particularly London, the place where reputations were made, and a shop window to the world. It was these lighter styles of blended whisky, still with an abundance of character for these new whisky drinkers, and with names and labels redolent of the wild and romantic Highlands and highlanders so much loved by Queen Victoria, that almost certainly would. Mature grain whiskies, with their sweet taste and creamy texture, took the edge off and softened the single malts; grains also acted as something of a catalyst when mixed with the malts, revealing new and otherwise hidden flavours. As the scale at which blends were being produced increased exponentially (Johnnie Walker, for example, claimed to have exported 51,000 cases in 1881; ten years later this figured had doubled) so blending became more complex, and the quest to maintain consistency more challenging.

The acquisition of whisky stocks became an imperative for blenders, but speculators had also entered the whisky market, seeing huge profits to be made as the drink's popularity continued to grow at home and abroad. The whisky rush had well and truly begun. A stream of distillery building also began as whisky production in Scotland grew almost threefold between 1870–1900 in order to satisfy 'the craze' for blended Scotch. Working at a scale undreamt of only a few years before, blenders perfected a process of assembling blends that was something akin to a jigsaw puzzle. Individual distilleries were grouped into broad regional styles such as Highland or North Country, Islay, Campbeltown, Lowland and finally grains. The whiskies were pre-vatted in these groups, and then the vattings finally blended together before being bottled. Of course, each blender had their own 'secret recipe', often comprising between 10-20 single whiskies, flexible enough to deliver the same overall character using a variety of whiskies, but distinctive enough to stand out against the plethora of brands on the market. Some blends had a very high malt content, others a very high grain content, but the consensus among blenders by the start of the twentieth century seemed to be that a ratio of something like 60 per cent grain to 40 per cent malt was the optimum to deliver the quality and character of blend that consumers were looking for.

HOW TO DRINK LIKE A DINOSAUR

By 1861 James Dunlop was selling his Mountain Dew in London; 'their blended whiskies are a great treat in sugar and boiling water' claimed one advertisement. Other early blenders sold their whiskies as 'Toddy Mixtures', promising 'gentlemen' that 'a glass of genuine toddy' would be guaranteed. Making toddies, a mixture of whisky, sugar, sometimes lemon juice, and hot water was one of the most popular ways of drinking whisky in the second half of the nineteenth century. Favoured by the 'respectable classes' over common dram drinking, toddies replaced punches (both whisky and rum) as social drinking gradually moved away from gatherings in the semi-public spaces of clubs and private dining rooms into the intimacy (and privacy) of the domestic environment. Here it was surrounded by paraphernalia and ritual. Toddy kettles, tumblers or rummers and muddlers for mixing the drink, spoons or ladles to transfer the steaming liquid to glasses for drinking. 'The implements for making toddy are household gods, which descend as heirlooms from one generation to another,' wrote Charles Dickens in 1865. 'The consumption of this national compound,' he continued, 'is a grand ceremonial, a solemn sacrifice to Bacchus, conducted with great state and circumstance.' The toddy was principally

Making toddies, a mixture of whisky, sugar, sometimes lemon juice, and hot water was one of the most popular ways of drinking whisky in the second half of the nineteenth century.

∧

an after-dinner drink, both the making and drinking a shared activity around the communal table.

The whiskies used for toddies were certainly strong – these early blends were normally bottled at proof or ten under, the equivalent of between 51-57 per cent abv today. They were heavy, oily and full-flavoured, no doubt with a distinct phenolic goût. But, properly made, a glass of toddy was a pleasing replacement for a bumper of sherry, which had fallen so out of favour in the 1870s and 1880s, the years when blended Scotch came to the fore. It also made an agreeable substitute for increasingly scarce cognac and brandy, as production in France was decimated by the spread of the phylloxera beetle that decimated vineyards in the Charente region and elsewhere. Supplies of quality cognac were constrained and prices steadily increased, while the UK market was flooded with cheap brandy, much of it adulterated with plain spirit imported from Hamburg. 'There is little doubt,' wrote the *Brewer's Gazette* in 1911, 'that Scotch whisky has to all intents and purposes killed brandy as a beverage in this country'. But whiskies to be drunk with mineral or soda water, which was becoming increasingly fashionable, needed to be lighter and fresher and so there was a distinct change in the style of blends in the 1890s and early 1900s. Blenders were looking for lighter styles of whiskies from the distilleries they used; as a consequence, distillers had to rethink the style and character of the whiskies they made. All of this was happening at a time when there were also significant changes in maturation regimes due to the shortage and prohibitive expense of genuine freshly emptied sherry casks (see page 57).

Times were certainly changing and the clock would never be turned back. Blended Scotch whisky, wrote a leading trade journal in 1915, 'is likely to hold its own so long as brands are well advertised and attention paid to quality ... blended whisky attracts the consumer largely, and Englishmen, in particular, have been gradually trained to the lighter styles of blend which they can drink with soda water – quite different to the taste of a quarter of a century

AN IRISHMAN AND A SCOTSMAN
WALK INTO A BAR

One of the other victims of the success of blended Scotch was Irish whiskey, which as we have seen with names like Kinahan's LL, Dunville's, John Jameson and George Roe, was enjoying considerable popularity in the 1850s and 1860s. 'The fact appears to be,' wrote a trade journal in 1881, 'that Irish whisky…is now suffering in its turn'. The Irish whiskey business was riven with jealousy, principally between the Dublin pot-still distillers on the one hand, and the Belfast distillers on the other, who produced grain whiskeys and blends. The four big Dublin firms (Powers, the two Jamesons and Roe) organised a propaganda campaign in the mid-1870s. This included pamphlets, books, articles in *The Times* and questions asked in parliament – decrying the use of Irish grain whiskey, or 'silent spirit' from Belfast for blending

Wine and Spirits Trade Record in 1898: 'the Scotch distillers supply that which people want, and the people buy it. The Irish supply what the people do not want, and consequently cannot sell it'.

with their whiskeys. They denounced this 'fictitious whiskey' in hysterical language, claiming its hazardous properties were not only due to the method of distillation, but also because it was often further adulterated with substances like creosote and methylated spirits. They also lambasted 'the dealers', those middlemen who had created successful brands by committing, according to their account, a criminal fraud against the public.

The large Dublin distillers feared being marginalised by the blenders, having failed to develop brands of note themselves. Their campaign backfired, the alarmist language provoking a consumer backlash against all Irish whiskey and further promoting the growth of Scotch. The continued refusal of the Dublin distillers to adopt either blending, or the marketing techniques so adroitly deployed by the Scots, led Adam Findlater (a leading figure in the Dublin trade) to lament their intransigence in an interview with the *Wine and Spirits Trade Record* in 1898: 'the Scotch distillers supply that which people want, and the people buy it. The Irish supply what the people do not want, and consequently cannot sell it'. He also excoriated the distillers and dealers of Belfast for producing low-cost and low-quality products that ruined the reputation of the category: 'there is no doubt that Belfast is at the bottom of the Irish disrepute'. Ironically having been bested for quality by the leading Scotch proprietary brands, much of the inferior Belfast whiskey started making its way to Scotland and England where it was used as a component in the very cheapest 'Scotch' blends and many 'tap whiskies' sold in pubs. This became something of a cause célèbre after the First World War, as attempts were made to resolve the legal ambiguities surrounding what could, and couldn't, be called Scotch whisky. This was finally resolved in 1939 after a test case led to the prosecution of several Glasgow firms for blending Irish whiskey and Scotch whisky together and selling it as Scotch, the judges at appeal delivering a clear ruling that only whisky distilled in Scotland could use the descriptor 'Scotch whisky'. This seems fair, given the name.

EIGHTEEN HOLES WITH AL CAPONE

The fate of Irish whiskey was now hanging in the balance and not even the thirsty throats of thousands upon thousands of Americans during the period known as Prohibition could restore its fortunes. From 1919–33 the manufacture and sale of alcoholic beverages in the United States was outlawed in what was known as 'the great experiment' to reform the morals and habits of a nation. This experiment proved to be a highly profitable business opportunity that many Europeans found hard to resist as whiskies, gins, rums and Hamburg grain neutral spirit (often used as a base spirit nowadays) found their way into this parched market through new and often improvised distribution channels. With the early emphasis always on exports to British colonial markets, blended Scotch had a slow start in the United States, not really gaining popular attention until the start of the new century. But during Prohibition it became the *jus du jour* at the tables of fashionable speakeasies, in middle-class dining rooms and at private parties, often served as a highball with dry ginger ale, a soft-drink whose popularity also increased enormously during this period. Although famous Scotch brands like Haig & Haig, Johnnie Walker and Dewar's suffered with everyone else from the sale of counterfeit products (some containing real Scotch 'cut' with other spirits, some simply raw spirit coloured and flavoured with creosote) the reputation of Scotch for quality was cemented during these years. At the start of Prohibition, whisky smuggling was described as 'the El Dorado of speculative financiers', as entrepreneurs and adventurers in London put together finances to purchase cargoes of Scotch, hire ships or even yachts and get them over to the edge of territorial waters where sales were made by the case to 'rum-runners' with high-speed boats who would navigate their prize back to dry land and sell it on to the bootleggers who serviced both bars and individual customers. This was the age of the Prohibition privateer, when fortunes could be easily made,

EVERYTHING YOU NEED TO KNOW ABOUT WHISKY

and easily lost. Later the business came to be dominated by large Canadian firms and American syndicates who legally shipped Scotch, mostly the brands of the Distillers Company, to Canada, the Bahamas, Mexico and other entrepôt ports before illegally moving it on to the United States. Scrupulously law-abiding, the Scotch blending houses made spectacular profits by turning a blind eye to the eventual destinations of these cargoes, as did the British government.

The bootleggers went to extreme lengths to ensure their cargoes made safe passage to their customers. Secret codes were used to exchange messages between boats to prevent interception by customs. Torpedoes loaded with bottles were fired from high-speed boats for the shore. Bottles were secreted in loaves of bread or hidden in trucks by fake cargoes of bricks. From the street-seller's heavy winter coat, lined on the inside with quart bottles, to the underskirts of society ladies whose corsetry shielded flasks from sight, there was almost nowhere free from a bottle of Scotch. The account of Francis Redfern, a lawyer and director of Johnnie Walker, of three months in the United States in 1929, told of a country where genuine Scotch whisky was available without restraint to visitors and citizens alike from arrival at the port of New York, in hotels, restaurants, trains, speakeasies and private houses. 'Everywhere I went,' he wrote, 'people sang the praises of the honest bootlegger. It was clear that no one enjoyed more respect than he, or stood higher in the social hierarchy.' Frequent visitors to London to discuss business with suppliers of the utmost respectability, the bootleggers were always welcome at places like Kate Meyrick's 43 Club, as men 'with tight lips but loose purse strings', though easily upset, when 'knives flashed or shots were fired'. Al Capone, a member of one of the large syndicates who bought whisky from the Distillers Company, is alleged to have visited Scotland secretly to play golf at St Andrews, Turnberry, Muirfield, accompanied by bodyguards especially recruited from Glasgow's notorious razor gangs. Meanwhile, within the Distillers

During Prohibition blended Scotch became the juice du jour and was often served as a highball with dry ginger ale, a soft-drink whose popularity also increased enormously throughout this period.

∧

Company in Scotland great scientific minds were set to work to explore the possibility that Scotch whisky might be made 'solid', thereby evading any Prohibition laws that only excluded the importation of 'liquors'.

Blended Scotch emerged from Prohibition as the luxury spirit of choice in the United States, which today maintains its position as one of the most important, and certainly most profitable, markets for both Scotch blends and single malts. It was about the same time that the idea of Scotch as a luxury, an aspirational drink and as a status symbol really began to take hold. This was a critical passport to its success in the twentieth century as it established itself in non-colonial markets. Scotch had a global footprint by 1900, but still very largely built on a British diaspora; it was after the Second World War that it really penetrated local populations and cultures. If Scotch had followed gold and diamonds around the early colonial markets, then it would follow oil and other prized minerals into Latin America, particularly in newly rich markets like Venezuela, where the conspicuous consumption of luxury imports was a mark of the arriviste. The commercial growth of economies like Japan, Taiwan and Thailand meant that blended Scotch was beginning to look eastwards by the 1950s.

Blended Scotch emerged from Prohibition as the luxury spirit of choice in the United States, which today maintains its position as one of the most important, and certainly most profitable, markets for both Scotch blends and single malts.

>

UN MÉLANGE DE DEUX, TROIS, QUATRE OU PLUS

If the 1960s and 1970s saw blended Scotch whisky emerge as
a truly global luxury drink of choice, then it also witnessed the
slow growth of single malts not just in the home market, but also
in Europe, particularly in Italy and France. A word here first on
the supposed 'singularity' of malts. The 'single' refers to a point
of origin, the product of a single distillery. It only in very rare
cases refers additionally to a single cask. Over 99 per cent of
all the single malt Scotches sold around the world are made up
from mixtures of a number carefully selected casks, sometimes
of different ages, but all produced at the same single distillery.
In many cases, those same blenders who may be responsible
for Ballantine's or Bell's are also charged with selecting the casks
that are blended together to produce these single malts. Here the
blender works with age and wood to establish the 'recipes' for
each of the single malts they produce. A malt may have an age
statement of ten years old, but that doesn't prevent the blender
from using something older as a 'top dressing' to make the whisky
really sparkle. Similarly the choice of wood is critical, the ratio

A word here first on the supposed
'singularity' of malts. The 'single'
refers to a point of origin, the
product of a single distillery. It only
in very rare cases refers additionally
to a single cask.

of seasoned sherry cask to bourbon cask to rejuvenated cask, and the ratio of first to second or third fill wood all have a huge influence on the final product. Occasionally in Scotland (though more typically in Canada and Japan), distilleries may also produce quite different distillates, which broadens the blender's palate of choice. The blender is the gatekeeper and guardian of the quality of everything that leaves their domain, whether it be single malt or blend. It's the blenders who determine the exact specification of the whisky to be made at each distillery; it's the blenders who oversee wood policy. When it comes to Scotch, despite all the romantic sentiment that's invested in distillers and distilleries, blenders really do call the shots.

Something else that shouldn't be lost sight of is the fact the character and style of the majority of single malt whiskies on the market have been shaped and defined by blenders over the past 100 years. It's only recently that any distillery has been able to devote the majority of its output to single malt bottlings; in the past all distilleries, independently owned or otherwise,

> The blender is the gatekeeper and guardian of the quality of everything that leaves their domain, whether it be single malt or blend. It's the blenders who determine the exact specification of the whisky to be made at each distillery. Despite all the romantic sentiment that's invested in distillers and distilleries, with Scotch, blenders really do call the shots.

∨

were dependent on selling their new make whisky, or 'fillings' to blending houses or speculators (who last century adopted the title of 'whisky brokers' in an attempt to make their business sound more respectable). Distillers had to make whisky in the style the blenders wanted, so as tastes slowly moved towards lighter and smoother whiskies, so the distillers had to follow. In a large company like Diageo or Pernod Ricard with multiple distilleries and many very famous single malts, the style of whisky produced at each distillery is strictly defined by the blenders in order to meet their requirements for blends like Johnnie Walker, Ballantine's or Buchanan's. It really is a truth that, despite the fact that so many recently proselytised malt whisky drinkers love to wear their disdain for blends on their sleeves like a badge of honour, the majority of the malt whiskies they like to enjoy today are a happy consequence of the success of blends. Blenders need the very best single malts to make the very best blended whiskies. It's their obsession with the quality and consistency of their blends that has given us the great single malts of today.

THE RETURN OF THE PRODIGAL SON

Single malts had never fully disappeared from the market; traditional wine merchants, and grocers like Gordon & MacPhail in Elgin, and wine merchants in major cities in England, kept the old traditions alive, blending their own whiskies and bottling small quantities of single malt under their own labels. In New York, the Macy's department store had only ever stocked one Scotch, Mortlach single malt, before Prohibition and supplies were resumed immediately after Repeal in 1933. But this was a rarity. As late as 1950 Sir Robert Bruce Lockhart lamented 'the passing of the single pot-still malt whisky'. In 1955 the Quill pub in Putney listed only 'Glenfiddich pure malt' among its 64 brands of Scotch. The malt whisky renaissance began in the heart of Speyside with

with innovations that echo much of what has been done with Scotch, and also with a refreshing and uncharacteristic degree of transparency. Normally the product of a single (and very large) distillery, the blends are made up from base spirit, normally distilled from corn in continuous stills, and flavouring whiskies, made in pot stills from rye, wheat and occasionally barley. This apparent simplicity hides the bewildering number of variables that come into play when the different maturation regimes and ages for the various base and flavouring whiskies are taken into account. Canadian Club is slightly different from other leading Canadian blends such as Wiser's or Crown Royal, as the constituent parts are mixed as new make spirit and matured or 'barrel blended' in a variety of carefully chosen wood types before being brought back together before bottling. This was a practice that was not uncommon in Scotland in the nineteenth century, particularly in the production of bulk blends for the pub trade. One thing that sets Canadian whiskies apart is that blenders are permitted by law to add other spirits or wines to their blends in strictly regulated proportions. Apparently very few do.

One thing that sets Canadian whiskies apart is that blenders are permitted by law to add other spirits or wines to their blends in strictly regulated proportions.

IT'S ALL SMOKE AND MIRRORS

Like Canadian whiskies, Japanese blends are almost always made up from different distillates from a single distillery, or only from distillates of distilleries owned by the same company. The practice of selling whiskies to competitors, or sometimes exchanging whiskies (known as 'reciprocals'), which is critical to the Scotch industry is unheard of in Japan. Japanese blenders do, however, use Scotch and other whiskies in blends destined for their domestic market and also in some exported products. As we have seen, the whisky industry in Japan is largely unregulated, although recently announced labelling regulations from the Japan Spirits & Liqueurs Makers Association will make it clear (at least from 2024) whether or not a consumer is buying whisky made, or rather distilled, in Japan. The mixing of domestic and other whiskies has not been against the law in Japan and blends produced there have profited in image, reputation and sales from the addition of bulk Scotch and other imported whiskies. The fact of the matter is that consumers have been misled for decades by Japanese producers; some might reasonablly expect an answer to the question 'what have we been buying?' Exports of bulk Scotch, both single malts and single grains, have boomed since the 1970s, and have particularly increased over the past ten years as supplies of domestic whiskies have been depleted due to the notable success of both Japanese blends and single malts in export markets. One might think that Scotch producers would have a care about exporting so much whisky to a market whose own product has been growing so determinedly in sales and reputation throughout the world. They certainly reacted with outrage when Suntory released one of their first whiskies in 1929 labelled, in English, as 'Suntory Scotch', 'Rare Old Island Whisky', aimed not just at domestic but also export Asian markets. While imitation may be the sincerest form of flattery, the wholesale adoption of the semiotics of Scotch was a real and present concern. But the glut of whisky in Scotland, known as 'the whisky loch', as a result of the astonishing growth in sales and production during the 1960s and early 1970s meant that beggars could not be choosers when it came to unloading surplus stocks. The great care for the integrity of the category claimed by some Scotch distillers seemed to evaporate in the face of commercial imperatives. Increasing overseas ownership and investment in Scotch businesses, some from Japan, has also tended to promote this apparent laxity.

The rule is, certainly until 2024, if you're going to buy a Japanese blended whisky, read the label carefully. Needless to say, however, the quality of the leading exported blends of Japanese whisky, like their much sought-after single malts, cannot be gainsaid. Hibiki 12 Year Old, partly matured in plum liqueur casks, was, until its withdrawal in 2015, one of the leading premium Japanese blends on the market. Non-aged replacements for the Hibiki range were launched as the age statement variants were withdrawn but today remain in short supply.

THEY'RE ALL JUST BLENDS

Try as you might, you are unlikely to find many people criticising the great champagne houses of France because their products are blended. Nor will you see people in restaurants shout in rage 'but they're all just blends' when the drinks trolley, loaded with cognacs with remarkably imaginative descriptions, comes to the table at the end of a meal. But Scotch just doesn't seem to be able to shake off the accusation that its blends are somehow inferior and secondary to the single malt whiskies. Think about the complexity of blending too long and you might actually wonder why a 12-year-old single malt would cost more than a 12-year-old blend. The new blenders, such as Compass Box, have a disarming indifference to these issues, embracing to a large extent transparency in place of secret recipes, and an artisanal language for their craft rather than one bogged down in marketing clichés. Refreshingly, founder John Glaser regards himself not as a 'master blender', another phrase borrowed from the French and first used by the Scotch industry in the late 1960s, but rather as a 'whisky maker', in the mould of American winemakers. Perhaps a little after the event, the large Scotch blending houses have adopted some, if not all, of Glaser's approach, in the same way that Canadian blenders began to lift the lid on their profession. At the same time this increasing willingness to talk meaningfully about blending has gone hand in hand with a whole range of innovations including heavily aged and high-priced special editions, cask finishing and even, in some cases, blends of whiskies of different nationalities, although not perpetrated as a fraud like the good old days, but as a value-enhancing gimmick. No matter what people may wish, nor how they might complain, blended Scotch remains the world's favourite whisky, a category led by brands such as Johnnie Walker, Ballantine's, Dewar's, Buchanan's, Chivas Regal and Grant's Stand Fast. When we asked some leading authorities about their favourite whiskies it was notable that Charlie MacLean, described by *The Times* newspaper as 'Scotland's leading whisky writer', a man who has probably tasted more whiskies than anyone else during his 40-year writing career, responded without hesitation: 'Johnnie Walker Black Label'. Regardless of the noisy newcomers, the brands that made the industry over one hundred and fifty years ago are still very much leading it, even if the companies that own the brands are now very different.

Think about the complexity of blending too long and you might actually wonder why a 12-year-old single malt would cost more than a 12-year-old-blend

THE BUSINESS
OF WHISKY

04

entered the Scotch world with the purchase of the BenRiach Company, with its three distilleries The GlenDronach, BenRiach, and Glenglassaugh. It also owns the newly built Slane distillery in Ireland. The formation of Diageo also caused a rupture in the relationship that had existed between Guinness and LVMH's Bernard Arnault, with his portfolio of champagnes and cognacs (in addition to the expensive handbags). The two had a cross-shareholding arrangement that was established in 1994 that gave LVMH over 20 per cent of Guinness, and Guinness around 35 per cent of joint venture Moët Hennessey. Rumours constantly circulated that Arnault, who once famously moored his yacht in the harbour at Oban and demanded to see 'his distillery', would make a move for Guinness, but none came. Arnault objected to the formation of Diageo and his shares were purchased by the new company for an eye-watering sum, some of which no doubt went towards his purchase of Glenmorangie and Ardbeg distilleries in 2004, since when they have been under the control of his luxury wine and spirits group. Diageo retained their interest in Moët Hennessey and so in theory own a third of both distilleries.

Three other overseas groups have also built up significant stakes in Scotch and other whiskies. In 2005 the Campari Group bought Glen Grant, a long-established single malt brand in Italy, and the Old Smuggler brand as Pernod disposed of assets in order to enable its Allied Domecq acquisitions to proceed. In 2009 Campari purchased, also from Pernod, the Austin Nichols distillery and the Wild Turkey and Russell's Reserve bourbon brands. In 2014 they added Forty Creek Canadian whisky to their portfolio. Few whisky businesses can have changed hands as much as Whyte & Mackay, with their eponymous blended Scotch and the Dalmore, Fettercairn and Jura distilleries. Passed around a bit like an unwanted orphan child, a 'colourful' parade of former owners include Sir Hugh Fraser's Scottish and Universal Investors, George Walker's Brent Walker, Tiny Rowland's Lohnro and Vijay Mallya's United Spirits. Whyte & Mackay are now

Top row, left to right: Ethel Robertson, Agnes Robertson, Elspeth Robertson, William Grant.

Middle row, left to right: Bernard Arnault, Patrick Ricard, Ernest Saunders, Samuel Bronfman.

Bottom row, left to right: William H. Ross, Shinjiro Torri, Vijay Mallya.

<

owned by the romantically named Alliance Global Group of the Philippines, through their subsidiary Emperador, makers of the world's bestselling brandy. In 2000 Whyte & Mackay sold its then-closed Islay distillery Bruichladdich to a consortium of investors fronted by wine-merchant Mark Reynier, who positioned himself, and the business, as whisky's David, firing indiscriminate slingshots at any perceived industry Goliath. Whisky enthusiasts, and some people who should have known better, fell for the romantic 'small guy, big guy' positioning, and everyone celebrated the reopening of another Islay distillery (following Ardbeg in 1997). With brilliantly deployed PR and marketing, and fronted originally by Reynier alongside Islay veteran Jim McEwan, the restored Bruichladdich, with a plethora of regular new releases, was a compelling proposition. But after twelve noisy years and a record-breaking number of distillery releases, the Bruichladdich single malt had mostly plateaued with growth largely coming from The Botanist, an early and very successful entrant into the burgeoning world of new gins. Cognac specialists Rémy Cointreau acquired the Bruichladdich business in 2012 as shareholders in the self-styled 'Progressive Hebridean Distillers' succumbed to a generous offer that ultimately only Reynier refused, choosing to leave the business to pursue equally noisy interests in rum and Irish whiskey. Rémy also own French distillers Domaine des Hautes Glaces and the Westland Distillery in Seattle.

CHARITY BEGINS AT HOME

In the midst of these corporates buying and selling brands like a crazed whisky collector on the secondary market, sits Edrington, owners of Macallan, Highland Park, Glenrothes and The Famous Grouse blend, a private company whose principal shareholder is a charity. Grouse, as it is generally known, became the largest selling blend in the UK in the 1990s, supplanting Bell's after years of dominance under former managing director Raymond Miquel. The Robertson Trust is a charitable foundation established in 1961 by three granddaughters of William A Robertson of Robertson & Baxter, noted Glasgow whisky brokers and blenders, and founder of Highland Distillers. The Trust uses the dividends from its majority holding in Edrington to support a variety of charities in Scotland, today focused on improving the lives of people and communities who have experienced trauma or poverty in Scotland; it's estimated to have given over £280 million to various causes since its creation. Edrington acquired the then privately owned Macallan in 1994 amidst some acrimony; Suntory retained a previously acquired 25 per cent share in the brand. It has subsequently disposed of distilleries such as Glenglassaugh, Tamdhu, Bunnahabhain, Old Pulteney and Glenturret, formerly the 'home' of its Famous Grouse brand, and the Cutty Sark brand, in order to focus on its 'core business'. It owns, along with Diageo, a half share in the North British Distillery in Edinburgh, and added Brugal rum to its brands in 2015. Under its stewardship Macallan has been transformed into a global luxury brand, with a multiplicity of special bottlings selling for eye-watering prices, regularly breaking records at auctions in London, Hong Kong and New York. Macallan has also become the darling of whisky collectors and speculators all over the world. However, some enthusiasts would argue that the style of Macallan's core expressions has changed noticeably over the past twenty years or so, and the brand has certainly forfeited the affections of some of these early and influential advocates. In 2018 it opened an audaciously designed new distillery at Macallan, built at a cost in the region of over £140 million, in the process closing stillhouses that dated back to the 1960s. In 2020, Suntory, with their pre-existing interest in the Macallan brand, purchased a 10 per cent share in Edrington; quite how Suntory's ambitions can be reconciled with a charitable trust remains to be seen.

The other major independent firm in Scotch is William Grant & Sons, established as distillers in Dufftown in 1887, owners of Glenfiddich and The Balvenie, Monkey Shoulder and Grant's Stand Fast. The first William Grant was trained in distilling at Mortlach distillery before setting up his own distillery on the other side of the village, fitting it out with patched-up stills discarded from Cardhu. The early business was effectively financed by William Williams & Co., bonders and blenders from Aberdeen, whose attempts to buy both Glenfiddich and Balvenie (built 1892) were firmly rebuffed. Instead, in 1897, Williams built the Glendullan distillery across the road. Glenfiddich was the leading single malt brand by a good length before the abolition of European duty-free in 1999 made a significant dent in its sales at the time, and it's now neck and neck with the Glenlivet for top spot, with Macallan coming up close behind. Grant's also own Kininvie Distillery, the recently built Ailsa Bay malt distillery, and Girvan grain whisky distillery, where Hendrick's gin is also distilled. They acquired the Tullamore D.E.W. Irish whiskey brand in 2010, and Drambuie in 2014. Family members still play an active role in the running of the business with ownership of the company spread across an extended network of family interests, shares being divided into ordinary and non-voting preference shares. The Grant Gordon family are claimed to be the wealthiest in Scotland as a result of their shareholding in the business. Of more modest fortunes are the Grants of Glenfarclas distillery on Speyside, a family-owned concern since 1865, famous for their sherried single malts.

The landscape of ownership and influence in the whisky business has changed significantly since the days of DCL dominance in the 1950s and 1960s, and change has been most dramatic over the past twenty years or so as global players have desperately tried to build up 'total beverage alcohol portfolios' in order to keep a place in the game. Once the playground of stock-market speculators it's now overseas drinks interests – French, Italian, American and Japanese – that have a significant say in the future of Scotch and other whiskies, although they mostly seek to obscure their ownership of much-loved distilleries and brands from consumers wherever possible. Sepia stories of long-standing traditions, inspirational founders and lifelong commitments to 'quality' are much preferred, but they can't hide the fact that the fate of much of the industry rests on decisions made in boardrooms in Paris, Chicago and Tokyo rather than Edinburgh or London. In some respects, this contrasts sharply with the burgeoning sector of new distilleries that have sprouted up not just in Scotland, but all over the world, over the past twenty years or so. There have been some 42 new distilleries commissioned in Scotland since 2004 – but many, like their corporate counterparts, are heavily dependent on overseas investment. North European, Russian and other investors have flocked to Scotland in search

Sepia stories of long-standing traditions, inspirational founders and lifelong commitments to 'quality' are much preferred, but they can't hide the fact that the fate of much of the industry rests on decisions made in boardrooms in Paris, Chicago and Tokyo rather than Edinburgh or London.

of projects to fund, the result being some very well-resourced business. Rarely can there have been a time of such excitement and energy in whisky making. Everyone wants to be a distiller, and everyone wants to try to be seen to be doing something new; craft and artisanal credentials are to the fore and 'funky' has emerged as a complementary tasting note. But the fact remains that whatever stories they may want to cloak themselves in, these new ventures are still in business to make money. That's why they are all anxious to turn convention on its head after a hundred and fifty years years or more and persuade consumers that drinking three-year-old whisky is really what aficionados should be doing.

THE EMPEROR'S NEW CLOTHES ...

Not all new distilleries in Scotland are the same. Indeed, if you look across the range some distinct typologies emerge. On the one hand there are the distilleries set up by drinks professionals, already vested to a greater or lesser degree in the business. Examples of this type would be Ardnamurchan, set up by independent whisky bottlers Adelphi and Ardnahoe on Islay, notable for its extensive tea room, built by bottlers Hunter Laing. Anthony Wills had a background in wine and whisky before setting up Kilchoman on Islay in 2005 with local farmer and food entrepreneur Mark French, whose fields would supply the distillery's barley. After a bit of a falling out, Wills took sole control of the business and bought the farm outright from the French family in 2015. Joint owner of retailers and bottlers The Whisky Exchange and Speciality Drinks, Sukhinder Singh, has been planning a distillery on Islay for the past seven years, which is now being built near Port Ellen. The very pretty Borders Distillery in Hawick was set up by a group of industry veterans, fronted by John Fordyce, formerly of Seagram. The Isle of Harris distillery, which like so many of these new enterprises is a very

At the end of the day, the whisky business is just that, a business, and everyone is in it to make money.

∧

community-focused operation, was set up by former Diageo and Glenmorangie executive Simon Erlanger. Makers of a very successful gin, Isle of Harris have yet to release any whisky on the market. Equally reticent when it came to selling young spirit were the owners of Daftmill distillery, whom one might put into a category of 'dreamers', people with a real passion for whisky but without the advantages of years of working in the business, and free from the pressures of hungry investors. The tiny Daftmill distillery in Fife opened in 2005 with little fanfare, named after the eponymous farm in which it sits. Like Kilchoman, and echoing the very first Highland distillers, the farm provides the barley for malting and distilling and takes by-products for its animals and land. Unlike many other new distilleries, the owners weren't in a rush to bring barely mature spirit to market, waiting ten years before releasing their new bottlings (which have been sold by hugely oversubscribed ballots). The group of nine friends behind Denmark's Stauning Distillery were also dreamers when they started up fifteen years ago, with no experience of whisky making; 'forget the whisky and open up a bakery instead' advised their bank when they went looking for finance. Such has been their success that Diageo stepped in with technical support and capital when they wanted to expand their distillery, but the owners have remained true to themselves with floor maltings and 24 small direct fired stills, albeit mostly all handcrafted at Diageo's coppersmiths in Alloa.

Of course not all dreamers realise their projects. Kingsbarns Distillery in Fife only came into being after the family behind the Wemyss Malts company stepped in after the original promoter had failed to raise all the capital required to build it. Ladybank Distillery, also in Fife, tells an even sorrier story; the heavily publicised Ladybank Company of Distillers Club was established in 2002 to 'add a new dimension to the world of Scotch Malt Whisky production'. The site: a dilapidated farm steading; 'members' invested over £750,000 on the promise of 'free' bottles and involvement in the running of the distillery, a bit like 'investors' in BrewDog with their rewards of 'free' beer. Although planning permission was granted, only a small amount of work was ever done on the buildings, the company folded and the so-called members never saw either their money or, needless to say, their 'free' bottles. Another unrealised dream was the equally heavily publicised Blackwood Distillery on the Shetland Islands, also established in 2002. A pipeline of products were developed under the Blackwood name (some by innovation guru Tom Jago, who had a hand in creating brands such as Baileys Irish Cream), gin, vodka, cream liqueur and the Muckle Flugga blend ('over-wintered' in a secret location on the island) but no distillery appeared despite the continuing round of positive PR stories always suggesting the contrary. Glossy brochures weren't enough to raise the capital needed, and what investors there were must have long given up any hope of seeing either a distillery, whisky, or their money. It is all about money in the end; the London Distillery Company (established in 2011), the first to distil whisky in England's capital for over a century, had more wacky ideas for distillates and ambitious plans than you could throw a stick at, but after several unsuccessful rounds of crowdfunding campaigns fell into administration in 2020. You can only take money off your mates for so long.

Brilliant marketing is what has made the whisky industry what it is today.

Alongside these doers, dreamers and occasional dodgy dealers are the new distilleries best described as marketing constructs, the products of slick thinking and word-perfect presentations, where what's really being sold is a concept, an idea, or a story craftily constructed to appeal to the less critically minded among 'the scotch whisky community'. That's not to suggest there's anything wrong with the whisky these distilleries produce; or that there's anything wrong with marketing – brilliant marketing is what has made the whisky industry what it is today. From the old to the new, Balvenie, Bruichladdich and Ballindalloch, all of these, even Bruichladdich with its brilliantly consistent 'anti-marketing marketing', are distilleries where ultimately the story is simply about making great whisky – marketing with substance *and* style, as some might argue it should be. At Ballindalloch, opened in 2014, a beautifully built little farm distillery close to the River Avon on the Macpherson Grant estate of the same name, everything is about distilling in the old fashion, with worm tubs and even water wheels. Compare and contrast with Lindores distillery for example, built in Fife in the grounds of the twelfth-century Lindores Abbey. The fictionalised narrative that gives the distillery its *raison d'être* concerns the famous Friar Jon Cor, long claimed to be the first recorded distiller in Scotland. The distillery's owners have placed Cor firmly at Lindores, making it, they say, 'the birthplace of Scotch whisky'. The whisky distillery Nc'nean claims to offer sustainable organic whisky, 'made by nature, not by the rules', guided by the spirit of the ancient goddess Neachneohain, 'a fierce protector of nature, she was never afraid to walk her own path'. This very twenty-first-century-minded distillery boasts some senior marketing types filed in from other huge corporations among its directors, and as such one might imagine there's no rule-breaking here. Nc'nean, and its highly praised new three-year-old whisky, is made exactly to the letter of the law, otherwise they wouldn't be able to call it Scotch whisky. But it's worth saying that sustainably minded practices are a cost-saving agenda long

adopted in the Scotch industry by small and large companies alike. For the record, they've also done a bit of a makeover on the 'gigantic and malignant' Neachneohain too.

Small versus big, David against Goliath, Jack climbing the giant's beanstalk; it's a weary trope that nonetheless never fails to seduce even the most rationally minded into rooting for the underdog. Some see in this apparent clash of little and large ideologies an existential crisis for whisky; others sense an opportunity to escape the dystopian landscape created by the corporates, an opportunity to return to, well, the good old days. When asked, our group of industry insiders welcomed the energy and enthusiasm of the new entrants, but few imagined that the explosion of small businesses would threaten the dominance of the large: 'The big companies will continue to be the locomotive that pulls the whisky train,' said Ingvar Ronde, 'but the small companies are needed to add an exciting diversity to the category. I see innovation coming from both types of companies – not just the small, so-called craft distilleries.' Balance, thought Dave Broom, was the key: 'a thriving small independent sector is vital, but so is the heft given by, well-run, larger firms. As for the shape, the days of Scotch's century-long hegemony are coming to an end. Greater choice, a wider spread of flavours and techniques. Exciting times.' The Whisky Exchange's Sukhinder Singh and writer and commentator Richard Woodard see positive advantages in newcomers coming into the business, 'the curiosity and inexperience of smaller distilleries can occasionally create superb liquid like the old days,' said Sukhinder; Richard hoped 'that smaller and newer companies can ask awkward questions,

The fictionalised narrative that gives the Lindores distillery, built in Fife in the grounds of the twelfth century Lindores Abbey its raison d'être concerns the famous Friar Jon Cor, long claimed to be the first recorded distiller in Scotland. The distillery's owners have placed Cor firmly at Lindores, making it, they say, 'the birthplace of Scotch whisky'.

∧

find new ways of doing things and, along the way, inspire the bigger operators to – using an unpardonable cliché – look to their laurels and renew themselves. Are the small companies here to stay? The jury is out: 'some will grow and may change the game' thought Serge Valentin of Whiskyfun.com, 'some will sell to larger "traditional" companies that will buy time, and many will just perish, sometimes very quickly because after all, that's the game.' Kurt Maitland agreed, 'I think big companies will still rule the day. They have the ability to learn from the moves that smaller companies make and the resources to survive mistakes (or buy the smaller innovators when necessary).' Being big brings responsibilities, so while Becky Paskin thought that 'future consolidation of distilleries is highly likely,' she was clear that 'they'll need to retain their independence and individual characteristics. More than ever, whisky distilleries are becoming a reflection of place, a quality that will be vital to their ongoing success.' 'The larger companies,' said Charlie MacLean, striking a warning tone, 'with their deep pockets and huge stocks, will survive, but they must not be complacent, especially those under foreign ownership with diversified interests (LVMH, Beam-Suntory, Pernod Ricard) managed by accountants and accountable to shareholders.'

Small versus big, David against Goliath, Jack climbing the giant's beanstalk; it's a weary trope that nonetheless never fails to seduce even the most rationally minded into rooting for the underdog.

DRINKING WHISKY

05

'The whisky flows like
a crystal stream they
say flows in heaven ...'

— Alabama 3, 'Speed
of the Sound of Loneliness'

Let no one be in any doubt. If the business of whisky is about money, then the drinking of whisky is about pleasure. It's about the enjoyment of a moment, shared or solus. It's about the *sgrìob*, the Gael's tingle of anticipation before a kiss of whisky on the lips. It's about those distant memories unlocked and brought into fresh focus by a chance aroma of gorse or peat or burnt Christmas cake or rice pudding. It's about an expansive world of flavour in a glass, from A to Z. It's about the sensory journey as the whisky passes across the palate, from sweet to hot to dry. It's about a mouth-coating and comforting warmth, and about a sometimes visceral finish as the spirit is swallowed. It's about companionship, in the moment or fondly remembered; about friends found and friends lost. It's about places, those destinations hidden in the glass that are brought to life in the act of drinking. It's about music, song and dance, about poetry and the magic of words. It's about sharing something special with generations of makers past, and makers present. It's about reflections on the day and reflections on a life. It's about safety and satisfaction. It's about pure hedonistic indulgent pleasure. If you're not enjoying your whisky, you really shouldn't be drinking it.

If you're not enjoying your whisky, you really shouldn't be drinking it.

IT AIN'T WHAT YOU DO, IT'S THE WAY THAT YOU DO IT ...

You may wonder why the world of whisky experts have chosen, with such enthusiasm, to appropriate the term 'dram' and 'dramming' to describe their Scotch whisky drinking adventures. It's not that the word isn't still used in Scotland, albeit it's a tad old-fashioned, but it conjures up nostalgic images of *Whisky Galore!* and *Dr Finlay's Casebook*, of Ma and Pa Broon on the back pages of the *Sunday Post*. A couthie world of simpler times where every household visit begins with 'come away in and we'll take a dram' and finishes with a 'wee deoch an doris', that final doorstep drink. But for the legions of international drinkers of Scotch who have adopted the word, 'dram' is almost like a passport or identity card that proves you're in the club rather than out of it. With a nod and a wink 'dram' elevates you above the brutish quaffer of this week's supermarket special offer. Connoisseurship with a devil-may-care *joie de vivre*. 'Unlike you English we only drink for the goût,' I remember an unsteady Frenchman telling me after a preposterous day of food, fine wines and fantastic *drams*. After which he gracefully fell to the floor in a posture that suggested practice rather than predicament.

> The great poet's instruction to 'take aff your dram' was not an invitation to embark on a thoughtful examination of the contents of a glass, it was a command to drink.

A dram, of course, is a medieval weight or measure. An apothecary's tool; Romeo's 'dram of poison'. It's certainly not a whisky-specific word, and it's certainly not Scottish. As it fell into more popular usage in Britain it became the common term for a small measure of spirits, rum, brandy, gin, whisky, or even sherry. Dram drinking, or dramming, was pervasive and pernicious, as this humorous account, allegedly from a Scottish minister, demonstrates:

Dramming is an odious vice, hateful to God and all decent bodies. It's no that I'll object to a drap now and then, in reason and moderation; but to be dram, dram, dram, dramming, morning noon and night – Oh it's just abominable! Ye may tak' a dram before breakfast, to keep the cauld out o' your stomach, and a dram after breakfast, just to settle the dried haddock, or kipper'd salmon; but ye maunna be always dram, dram, dram, dramming. And I'll no object to a dram maybe at noon, when ye're over weary of fasting, and a dram before dinner for a whet, and a dram after dinner for the digestion is a dram in season, and a dram after tea's what no one will tak amiss, for tea's a poor lap and hurtful to the stomach without a qualification; but as for dram, dram, dram, dramming everlastingly, it's a sair and brutal sin. Then ye may tak a wee drappie before supper, to gie a kick to the appetite, and twa drams after it, for supper's apt to lie heavy without a moderate stimulus; and then ye'll hold out, I expect, till next morning without anything more, but maybe a cup at your bed-head, in case ye be dry in the night. This ye may do, for it's all in moderation; but dinnae be aye dram, dram, dram, dramming – for it's a hateful custom, and nae Christian body should practice it.

— Unknown Scottish Minister, quoted in *The Atlas*
    26 October 1826

Working-class men and women in towns and cities took their drams in dram-shops, gentlemen in luncheon bars or clubs, their wives more discretely in drawing rooms and parlours. But wherever it was done there was an urgency about dramming that allowed no room for relaxation or reflection. Aficionados of the dram shop were experts in perpendicular drinking: the great poet's instruction to 'take aff your dram' was not an invitation to embark on a thoughtful examination of the contents of a glass, it was a command to drink. Dramming was like drinking shots, the dram to be consumed as quicky as possible, often because the liquor served in dram shops was of the basest quality. The historical reality of dram dramming is far away from the way the word is used today.

OLD FASHIONED

Rocks glass or tumbler

60ml bourbon or rye
10ml sugar syrup
3 dashes bitters

Garnish: orange zest twist

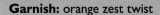

— Stir 25ml bourbon or rye into a glass with two ice cubes.
— Add sugar syrup, bitters, two more ice cubes and stir.
— Add the remaining bourbon or rye and more ice cubes, and stir to taste.

Working-class men and women in towns and cities took their drams in dram-shops, gentlemen in luncheon bars or clubs, their wives more discretely in drawing rooms and parlours.

<

THROUGH A GLASS DARKLY

Most people drink their whisky from a classic tumbler.

∧

The Whisky Exchange's 'Perfect Measure' glass.

∧

When it comes down to it there are really three or four ways you can drink your whisky. First there's the forensic tasting; the considered analytical consumption that might follow a semi-formal process, including not one but several whiskies for comparative purposes, and may involve taking notes or even scoring whiskies. It's called an organoleptic assessment. Then there's the more hedonistic approach, which is more about the moment than the marking, although it doesn't preclude some appreciation of the liquid in the glass. A third way is in a whisky cocktail increasingly fashionable as an at-home indulgence. And finally there's the shot, the dramming, the get-it-over-with-as-soon-as-possible sort of drinking. Of the first three no one is better than another – each is a specific occasion taking a different path to whisky paradise. But each presents the new drinker with a particular dilemma. What glass should I use?

There is no shortage of whisky glasses to choose from. Indeed, barely a month goes by without another new glass coming on to the market, claiming to be just the very best thing for nosing, tasting or drinking whisky. You need to be aware, if you're going to start buying and drinking whisky seriously, that you'll need to run a separate budget for accessories: kit, the glasses, water jugs, cocktail equipment, notebooks, tasting books, tasting guides and, of course, the T-shirts. The real professionals, the blenders whose job it is to smell (or 'nose'), taste and assess whiskies day in, day out, almost all use what are called standard ISO nosing glasses, small copita or sherry-style glasses with a short stem and bulbous bottom, which narrows to the mouth, allowing aromas in the glass to concentrate. They might have gradations, and they might be tinted (normally dark blue) to prevent the colour of the liquid influencing the taster's judgement. Sometimes blenders might use a watch glass (like the glass covering the face of a watch) to cover the glass to ensure none of the aromas are lost. A more popular, more drinkable, and less fragile version of the ISO is the Glencairn glass, created by Raymond Davidson in 2001, and now almost ubiquitous at whisky festivals and distillery visitor centres throughout the world. Somewhere in between these two is the 'Perfect Measure' tasting glass, designed by Sukhinder Singh and also manufactured by Glencairn. Always have a couple of one of these three in your cupboard. Always make sure they are clean, and as with any glass smell them before you fill them, just in case. What one might call drinking glasses range from the very traditional cut-glass crystal tumblers to the aesthetically overcharged Norlan glasses. Glassmakers Riedel offer their 'vinum' version of a nosing glass and they also have a range of stemless wine tumblers that are excellent for whisky cocktails like a Manhattan or Old Fashioned. Of course, some people like to serve all their cocktails in Martini glasses; it's all down to choice. Classic highball glasses are, not surprisingly, perfect for whisky highballs. At the end of the day most people will choose a glass that suits their pocket, and crucially their hand. The ergonomics of glassware are just as important as 'smellability'. And don't be afraid of having a favourite glass, even if it's the one you bought at a charity shop years ago. Everyone does.

The world-famous Glencairn tasting glass.

∧

There is no shortage of whisky glasses to choose from. Indeed, barely a month goes by without another new glass coming on to the market, claiming to be just the very best thing for nosing, tasting or drinking whisky.

PERFECT MANHATTAN

Coupe or rocks glass

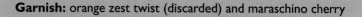

60ml bourbon
12.5ml sweet vermouth
12.5ml dry vermouth
2 dashes Angostura bitters

Garnish: orange zest twist (discarded) and maraschino cherry

— Stir all the ingredients with ice and strain into a chilled glass.
— Squeeze the orange twist over the glass and discard.

When it comes to glassware, our experts seemed to agree on one thing above all: this is surely the question most likely to instigate a bar brawl between whisky enthusiasts. The real tasters, when tasting, seemed to have a preference for the standard ISO copita (which some also chose for social drinking), the Glencairn, and the 'Perfect Measure', of which Sukhinder Singh had to say 'after many years in the industry it is something I am very proud to have developed'. Everyone agreed that the Glencairn scored highly for robustness and practicality – particularly at whisky festivals, where it is de rigueur to hang one of these glasses from one's neck by a lanyard, in much the same way as a bell would hang from the neck of a prize cow. Emmanuel Dron, of Singapore's The Auld Alliance bar, which stocks over 1,500 whiskies, some of which date back to the nineteenth century, chose a Riedel Vinum cognac glass; some liked the Riedel whisky glass whose 'wide tulip shape allows the heady alcoholic vapours out while still retaining the more delicate aromas', although one confessed 'I can only use it in private as it looks silly in my hand'. Hand feel, the ergonomics of the glass was clearly an important factor, as was sentimentality. 'A glass tumbler with a heavy bottom,' said Becky Paskin, 'I love the weight of it in my hand'. Drinks writer and editor Richard Woodard loved 'the feel of a solid, weighty tumbler pressing into my palm, but it's not made for drinking pleasure'. Rob Allanson said 'my favourite is a glass that I used to have a set of, but now only have one. It is a crystal tumbler from the 1940s but it is really small. It fits just about one dram and a splash of soda in it. Perfection'. Billy Abbott's choice was also tinted with nostalgia: 'if I'm in full-on, old-fashioned whisky-drink mode, then a chunky Stewart Crystal tumbler – it's an identical cut pattern and size to the one I received for my twenty-first birthday from my flatmates of the time. They were the first to realise that whisky might end up being quite important to me.' Few were as catholic as Dave Broom, 'for drinking? I don't care!'

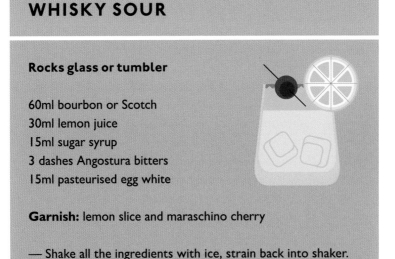

WHISKY SOUR

Rocks glass or tumbler

60ml bourbon or Scotch
30ml lemon juice
15ml sugar syrup
3 dashes Angostura bitters
15ml pasteurised egg white

Garnish: lemon slice and maraschino cherry

— Shake all the ingredients with ice, strain back into shaker.
— Dry shake (no ice) and fine strain into an ice-filled glass.

'IT'S JUST LIKE LICKING THE INSIDE OF A HEAVILY USED ASHTRAY'

If you're going to taste whisky, and maybe even write some notes about it, then you need to understand the language of whisky flavour, which applies to nosing as much as it does tasting. Of course ordinary people like you and me have quite a limited vocabulary when it comes to describing whisky. Many drinkers feel rightly quite accomplished if they can describe the liquid in their glass as smooth or rich, sweet or dry, spicy or smoky; and there's nothing wrong with any of these words. One way to articulate what you're tasting further is to relate the tastes you experience to something you're familiar with; 'it tastes like …' or better still, 'it reminds me of …'. It's Proustian I suppose, the remembrance of things past can help you define a taste or flavour in the present and drill down to a quite specific descriptor. You might start with 'it reminds me of apples' and end up with 'the burnt sugar crust on a baked apple' if you let your memory and imagination work hand in hand. In order to work with a standardised language, blenders tend to break whisky character down into groups of core aromas or flavours, which are often represented on a wheel, the main groups at the centre radiating out to more detailed descriptions on the circumference. In doing so they have developed an extensive lexicon of whisky words, something that writer and taster extraordinaire Charlie MacLean has worked on for many years. So, six core flavour or aroma groupings could be malty, fragrant, fruity, pungent, woody and peaty. Here 'apple' might appear as a subsection of malty (green apple), fragrant (fresh apple) and fruity (stewed apple). Identify the type of apple you can smell, and you can then track it back to a core aroma. At first sight it might seem preposterous to suggest that you might smell or taste green bananas, chocolate, pork sausages or kippers in a glass, but believe me if you stick with it you can. If you need help with words find a flavour wheel to use, like the one printed in Charlie

MacLean's *Malt Whisky*. And while you can discover a lot of these flavours yourself, tasting with a friend or group of friends, discussing and building these flavour profiles together is a much better, and often a more enjoyable, way of doing it. Everyone just has to realise, there are no wrong answers. At the end of the day what you smell and taste, is what you smell and taste. Not everyone will taste the same things, not everyone can taste the same things – some people – even the most accomplished tasters, have blind spots to certain aromas or flavours.

The procedure for nosing and tasting is quite straightforward, and do remember, if you're doing this at home then do make sure it's fun. There's nothing worse than a group of stern-faced over-earnest whisky geeks gloomily tutting and fretting their way through a group of samples like frustrated musicians in search of the lost chord. Have a clean nosing glass for each whisky you're going to try and some chilled water for dilution (some people make a fetish of the water they use for diluting whisky; for a tasting it should be still and cool, that's all). You might have a pipette to measure the amount of water you add to your samples. Notebook, pencil, some dry unsweetened biscuits to nibble between each whisky, and possibly some loud rock 'n' roll music. This is an organoleptic tasting – all the senses should come into play.

Everyone just has to realise, there are no wrong answers. At the end of the day what you smell and taste, is what you smell and taste.

Take a look at the bottle. The label will tell you which country the whisky has come from, if it's a single malt whisky it should tell you which distillery it's from, it may carry an age statement (remember, this will be the age of the youngest whisky in the bottle) and it will also tell you how strong the whisky is. These pointers may all start to shape your expectation of what you might find in the glass, which can be helpful, although many professional tasters would prefer to nose and taste 'blind', with no clues as to what they may be trying. One thing people sometimes look for is the 'bead' of a whisky, sometimes an indicator of strength. If there's some headroom in the bottle, give it a good shake (with the cork or screw cap on of course) and you'll notice bubbles forming on the surface of the liquid. Simply put, the more bubbles, or the greater the 'beading', and the longer they last, the stronger the whisky. Next, pour a small measure into your glass and take a look. The colour may give you some indication of age, and in a single malt possibly what sort of cask or casks the whisky has been matured in. But note that many blenders and bottlers use something called spirit caramel, a flavourless substance allowed by law, that helps them deliver a consistent colour from batch to batch, so it's always possible the colour may have been adjusted. It's fair to say this is a festering sore of a subject, with some purists (often the same ones who say 'bring back paxarette') arguing that it should not be allowed. It is certainly true that the dark colour of those cheapest of blends on a supermarket shelf is likely to have its origins in burnt sugar rather than time in the cask, but the majority of bottlers use it very sparingly just to ensure consistency, and analysis has shown it is undetectable in most of the whiskies it is used in. So, look at the colour, and look at the body of the whisky too. Swirl it round the glass. Does it have a degree of viscosity? Is it sticking to the side of the glass, or quickly returning to the bowl? If it's 'sticky' then that might tell you something about the texture of the whisky when you taste.

Now to the nosing. Sniff it carefully – if you can, keep your mouth open when you do, like the wine tasters do on TV.

Remember the whisky at this point will be at least 40 per cent abv, and possibly more. So don't let your nose linger too long over the glass or you'll get 'nose burn', which will impair your sense of smell. Pull away, then go back to the glass and sniff again, repeating two or three times. Is the nose open, or is it closed? Assertive or shy? If the former, you may begin to pick out some of the whisky's particular aromas, which will reveal themselves in a layered way each time you go back to the glass. If you can pick out something like smoke, or vanilla, cereal or fruit then you're doing pretty well. The more you can work on these individual elements, the more you can piece together the jigsaw of the whisky's character. But if all you're getting is 'smooth', then that's fine too. Everyone loves smooth whisky. Now you're ready to take a small taste, where you need to consider a number of things. What is the whisky's texture, and its mouthfeel – does it have a viscosity, is it coating the inside of your mouth, is it as tasters sometimes say 'chewy'? Also try to think how the taste develops from that initial encounter with your lips – usually sweet – to your palate, where you might sense some drying and possibly bitterness. And then the 'finish'. Short or long? Do the whisky's flavours disappear as soon as you swallow, or do they linger, even develop? Is there a 'catch', a sudden strong farewell like the famous peppery finish of a 10-year-old Talisker?

At this point, if you want to keep with the jigsaw analogy, you may just be starting to see in the mass of pieces the sky from the sea, and the sea from the land, with odd flashes of structure or colour, a beach, a building, a copse of trees? Hopefully you haven't decided to put the whole lot back in the box. Now repeat the nosing and tasting exercise, but this time with the addition of a little water. That's the way you should always do it for a forensic tasting; first neat, then with water. At full strength of 40 per cent, the alcohol, the ethanol, can get in the way of the flavours; at cask strength of 50 per cent or more the whisky might do little other than cauterise the palate, leaving little room for discernment, so sip with care. While freelance tasters and writers will tell you

Tasting whisky is actually a multi-sensory process; looking, smelling (or 'nosing') and then finally tasting.

>

all sorts of nonsense about how to taste whisky, the fact of the matter is that the real professionals tend to reduce whiskies down to around 25 per cent abv (that's a little less than half water to half whisky) when they're trying to assess their character, their strengths and flaws. If you're a novice, unused to drinking whiskies at higher proofs, this is probably a good place for you to start too, although with practice you might find you prefer it higher. So, with the addition of water, aim for a strength like that and then go through the nosing and tasting again, slowly. You should find that the whisky becomes more expansive in every way, the aromas stronger and clearer, and possibly quite different from the undiluted version, and the tastes and flavours more clearly drawn. Just like the jigsaw; now you should be able to see both the distant horizon and the shore, an unthought of wind farm out at sea, and on land both buildings, wood and the trees. If you are using a notebook, scribble down your thoughts – it's best done in the moment, although having done this many tasters might leave the sample for a while, allowing it to further develop in the glass, before returning to it once more, like that wretched jigsaw puzzle on the kitchen table.

PENICILLIN

Rocks glass or tumbler

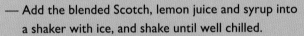

50ml blended Scotch
20ml lemon juice, freshly squeezed
20ml honey-ginger syrup
10ml Islay single malt

Garnish: candied ginger

— Add the blended Scotch, lemon juice and syrup into a shaker with ice, and shake until well chilled.
— Strain into a rocks glass over fresh ice, and top with the Islay single malt scotch.

THE TYRANNY OF THE TASTING NOTE

If you managed to stick through the process then what you should end up with in your notebook are what the industry likes to call 'tasting notes'. Now, quite who wrote the first tasting notes for whisky remains to be seen. Certainly Alfred Barnard, one of the original whisky writers, barely mentioned the taste of the whiskies produced at the distilleries he visited the length and breadth of the Kingdom in the mid-to-late 1880s. We have already seen that early retailers were more than happy to shower their whiskies with superlatives like 'Fine', 'Very Fine' and 'Super Fine', and by the 1860s and 1880s they liked to draw attention to the 'full flavour' of their stocks, without talking exactly about what the flavours were. When writers were a little more specific about flavours they tended to focus on one thing, their views often strikingly contradictory. An advert for Loch Lomond whisky in 1870 claimed it 'possessed all the agreeable characteristics that pertain to Scotch Whisky without its too often disagreeable smokiness'; on the other hand *Illustrated London News* praised 'that peaty flavour which is so much prized by lovers of Scotch whisky'.

In the nineteenth century the trade press saw flavour, and more importantly variety of flavour, as being the key to Scotch's success: 'we are inclined to think' wrote *Ridley's Wine and Spirits Trade Circular*, 'that the public taste for Scotch will be of a much more enduring character than that for the Irish whisky, the several makes of which differ but slightly in style and flavour. Whereas Scotch makes, whether sold "entire" or as one of the leading components of a blend, command each of them their circle of adherents'. These relative merits of individual distilleries were often claimed: 'the Clynelish whisky is undoubtedly not to be surpassed by the Brackla, or even the pristine Glenlivat', it was written in 1850, but never explained. Occasionally someone did venture into the more lyrical style of writing to which we have today become, if anything, somewhat over-accustomed:

> The Oban distillery is the oldest in the Highlands, perhaps the world. The claim of the Oban Distillery to produce the Finest Scotch Whisky goes uncontested … At the Oban Distillery the 'mountain dew' comes in at one door – water – straight from the hills, and goes out at the other door – whisky – for shipment at the Steamboat Quay. The water comes down

from moss and mountain, vitalised with the ozone of the hills, fragrant with heather, sweet with wild thyme, and laden with the aroma of a thousand flowers, whose delicate bouquet is preserved in the spirit …

— *Burnley Express and Advertiser,* 14 March 1885

Even when single malt whiskies came back into favour, the language of flavour, of tasting notes, was somewhat absent from marketing communications which singularly focused on the 'malt' credential; Glenfiddich was smooth and mellow, a little later Macallan was a 'voluptuous gold', billowing with aroma, and billowing with flavour, with sherry and sherry casks somewhere in the mix but not explained. When flavour did rear its ugly head it tended to be in the columns of wine writers like Peta Fordham and Jane MacQuitty who increasingly stepped over into the whisky world in the absence of any whisky specialists. At the same time the Scotch industry was developing its own language for describing whisky, one might have thought somewhat belatedly; the independent Pentlands Scotch Whisky Research company began developing possibly the first flavour wheel for whisky in 1979, albeit intended for 'the trade' rather than consumers. At the same time the BBC TV series *Food & Drink*, first broadcast in 1982 had awakened a latent appetite in the British public for taste talk, famously from wine writer Jilly Goolden. Nonetheless Philip Morrice's *The Schweppes Guide to Scotch*, published in 1983, was characteristically reticent about flavour with rarely more than two descriptors allowed for any given whisky, if at all: Glenmorangie was 'surprisingly light and fragrant', Glenfarclas 'dry and mature' and the much-admired Longmorn bottled with a 'dry and nutty' taste. Subverting this stolidness the maverick independent bottlers the Scotch Malt Whisky Society began as an informal tasting panel around founder Pip Hill's kitchen table in the early 1980s, dreaming up descriptors that were not for the faint-hearted. When the Classic Malts were launched by United Distillers in 1987, taking some considerable inspiration from the success of new world wines and putting whisky regions in place of terroir, accessible tasting notes were at the fore of their consumer marketing. Wallace Milroy's *Malt Whisky Almanac*, a compendium of tasting notes, was published in the same year. Michael Jackson, who had already established a reputation writing about both the production and the taste and flavours of beer, published his *Malt Whisky Companion* in 1989. Tasting notes were here to stay; at the same time, regardless of the role played by these early women wine writers, the status of the patriarchal whisky expert, handing down unquestionable wisdom from on high like Moses might commandments, dictating 'good taste' was established.

The tenure at the top for these gurus of goût was relatively short-lived as the Internet rapidly democratised the world of tasting notes, at least for those with high-speed broadband connections and sufficient disposable income to invest in the never-ending flow of new bottlings, initially mostly Scotch single malts, but now including a plethora of whiskies from all over the world. So while the undoubted expertise of tasters like Charlie MacLean and Dave Broom are still highly sought after by distillers and blenders anxious to get external validations of their products, and while their tasting notes still find their way into publicity materials and print magazines, consumers are just as likely to be guided by the tasting notes on websites from non-professionals (some of whom, as we shall see, have a huge cult following) or of a 'friend' on one of the many whisky-related Facebook groups or elsewhere on social media. In fact, the Internet is full of people only too keen to tell you exactly what they think of the latest release of Glen Cliché, or Granddad's Old Predictable. So, once you've finished your forensic tasting, and have your tasting notes written in your notebook, you can easily (if so desired) add them to the digital fray. Undoubtedly the best place to go if you do want to share your thoughts is Whiskybase, a remarkable online community of over 100,000 enthusiasts from around the world (around three quarters of whom are men) who regularly post their thoughts on new (and old) bottlings. At the time of writing they have contributed over 300,000 individual tasting notes on the site and records of over 160,000 different bottlings.

IT'S TIME FOR A DRINK – AT LAST!

If you've done with tasting then it must be time for drinking, or in other words some purely hedonistic enjoyment of whiskies without any recourse to pen, pencil or paper. Contrary to many people's expectations there are no rules or regulations about how you must drink whisky, although there are possibly some guidelines. There are also some widely held myths; false truths that seem to be deeply rooted in popular belief around the world, the origins of which are not always clear. The most widely known is the assertion that you should never add anything to your whisky. Well, for most normal people a drink of 40 per cent abv is pretty strong, let alone one at 50 per cent or more. Remember that most beers are around 5 per cent abv, wines between 12–14 per cent. The regular strength of whisky, as we have seen, is almost too much to taste; it can certainly take the pleasure out of whisky if you're not used to it. It can make drinking whisky seem like an ordeal, like some medieval test or challenge to see who's toughest, who can really take it. Sadly, this is how some enthusiasts seem to like it, believing that to add just a splash of water to your drink is somehow defiling the dignity of Scotland's national drink – ignoring the fact that most Scots take their Scotch with a dash of lemonade. It is, of course, all down to personal preference. Water can be whisky's best friend; it tames the fire, it 'opens up' both the aromas and flavours in the spirit that ethanol will keep hidden. Adding water to a smoky whisky, for example, is like damping down a fire. The smokiness will be amplified. Water will also find sweetness in the glass too. Put simply, added judiciously, it can often make drinking whisky more fun. However, there are some whiskies which are so delicate that even small amounts of water can kill both aroma and flatten the taste. This can be particularly true of very old whiskies, either old in age, or long in the bottle. So always use water with care, and remember, at the end of the day it's about how *you* like to drink *your* whisky. Perhaps consumption of whisky would double if only drinkers around the world could be persuaded that adding water really was okay.

Some writers and critics like to point the finger at what they call 'the industry', claiming it is 'the industry' that's responsible for propagating these myths, and creating these rules in the minds of consumers. Yet if you look back at well over a hundred years of advertising you'll quickly see that water or the soda syphon is always close to hand when drinking scenes are portrayed. As we know, respectable drinking in the good old days was all about mixing; whisky punches and whisky toddies, and then later sodas, seltzers and 'potash waters' were the preferred mixers of the day. In the 1890s John Walker & Sons did joint promotions for their brands with the Rosbacher mineral water company; Schweppes and others widely advertised their products as being most suitable for drinking with Scotch. Indeed, it could probably be argued that it was the ubiquity of whisky and soda that made Scotch so popular in the late Victorian and Edwardian era because the addition of a mixer made the drink more accessible, just like adding water (or soda for matter) does today. But of course some people in the past (and sadly in the present too) despised this popularity. The polemicist Aeneas MacDonald had nothing but contempt for the whisky and soda drinker; for him the whisky and soda was the nadir of the national drink he almost deified. Those who defiled its purity were fit for only scorn and derision. MacDonald had form when it came to extreme political views and those notions of racial purity that gained so much currency in the 1930s, and he managed to integrate Scotch into this distasteful

Weltanschauung, or 'world view'. He wasn't the first to suggest that the rise of blended Scotch whisky had coincided with, if not been responsible for, the decline or disappearance of an imagined race of noble highlanders; principled Caledonian virtue overtaken by casual cosmopolitan vice. Some argued that the increased availability of canned and bottled food and preserves had had a similarly demoralising effect. The purity of a nation diluted; views that became quite commonplace among the literary and intellectual elite of Scotland during the so-called Scottish renaissance of the mid-twentieth century. MacDonald, and many other influential figures of the period, wanted to keep 'real' Scotch as the preserve of a privileged and private club, the complete opposite of the common man's drink so lionised by Robert Burns. And of course real Scotch meant no water, just like it does for some of today's more extreme whisky drinkers. No enfeeblement of the national life-blood. No water, no ice, no lemonade, no mixing, whether for sentimental or more sinister reasons. It's these people who should be thanked for the so-called rulebook of Scotch.

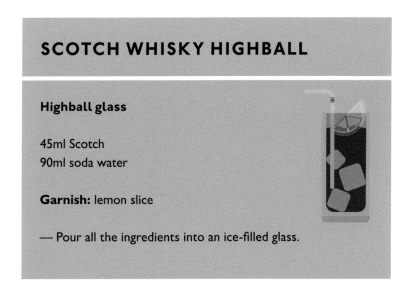

SCOTCH WHISKY HIGHBALL

Highball glass

45ml Scotch
90ml soda water

Garnish: lemon slice

— Pour all the ingredients into an ice-filled glass.

RIP UP THE RULEBOOK

Whisky is enjoyed around the world in any number of ways. With water, with a few cubes of ice, with crushed ice (American style), with hand-carved ice-balls in Tokyo's Shibuya district. Jack and coke all over the world, Scotch with cola in Spain, with green tea in China, with coconut water in Latin America. Then there's the whisky highball, allegedly invented by Tommy Dewar during his travels in the United States in 1892, a long drink of Scotch and soda with ice, or as became ubiquitous during Prohibition, with ginger ale. Suntory revived the whisky highball a few years ago, with a tap-serve for bars and canned pre-mixes available too; they also heavily promoted 'mizuwari', a long, chilled whisky with water. Neither entirely novel, but Japanese whisky disciples hailed both as breakthrough innovations. Today the whisky highball is a recruitment platform for some of the world's leading blended whiskies, such as Johnnie Walker, who are investing huge sums of money around the world in an attempt persuade new drinkers that Scotch isn't 'difficult', that it's not hidebound and, most importantly, that it's about having fun. A few years ago a number of brands, both Scotch, Canadian and American whiskies, were trying to do the same with the boilermaker. According to the late Gary Regan, the origins of this 'drinking ritual' rest with Pennsylvania steelworkers, quenching their thirst after a day's work with a shot of whisky followed by a more considered glass of ale. As one might have expected, Gary suggested there was fun to be had in matching styles of beer with styles of bourbon. Drop the glass of whisky into the beer and you have a 'depth charge'. It's doubtful that idea would have been greeted with great enthusiasm in the glorious bars of Glasgow's Dumbarton Road, once heaving with shipyard workers at the end of shift enjoying the Scottish equivalent, a 'hauf an a hauf'. Don't expect the whisky killjoys to approve of such pleasures. And, whatever you do, don't mention whisky cocktails to them. Alessandro Palazzi, the great

Martini maker from London's famed Duke's bar, was once asked to make a whisky negroni in front of an international audience of the most extreme malt whisky enthusiasts at Lagavulin Distillery during Islay's famous whisky festival, the Feis Ìle. The equivalent, one might think, of being asked to put one's head into a lion's mouth. Needless to say the great maestro carried off the task with considerable aplomb, but as he did so many of his audience cradled themselves and rocked to and fro, exhibiting signs of great distress. Apparently some wept when the Lagavulin was mixed with Campari and sweet vermouth.

BLOOD AND SAND

Coupe glass or martini glass

25ml Scotch
25ml cherry brandy liqueur
25ml sweet vermouth
25ml fresh orange juice,
    preferably blood orange

Garnish: orange zest twist

— Shake all the ingredients with ice and strain into
   a chilled glass.

It's not that mixed drinks, or whisky cocktails, are a new thing. American Bars and 'Yankee drinks' were common enough in England by the middle of the nineteenth century, particularly in the London pleasure gardens at Vauxhall and Cremorne, and events like the Great Exhibition of 1851 and the International Exhibition of 1871. In the meantime pubs in London and, perhaps surprisingly, Liverpool were reshaping themselves as American bars, promising gin slings, cocktails, stonefence, brandy smash, mint juleps, sherry cobblers and more. These new drinks also obtained early royal patronage. When the Prince of Wales visited the United States in 1860 it was hoped 'that he will have an opportunity of distinguishing between the real mint-juleps, brandy cocktails, phlegm-cutters, eye-openers, corpse-revivers and other celebrated American drinks, and the base imitations of them which we compound in this country'. In June 1870 the Prince hosted 'one thousand of the highest members of the aristocracy' at a 'Royal Fete' at Chiswick House in West London, where he 'improvised an American Bar where mint-juleps, brandy smash, cocktails, and other American beverages were served to curious enquirers'. In 1887, of course, he is said to have created The Prince of Wales cocktail, made with a base of rye whiskey. By this time no fashionable hotel or theatre in the capital was without an

For women in particular, cocktails represented a downhill path to moral turpitude, with many media outlets taking the rather strong view that a habit of cocktails quickly led to a habit for something altogether much stronger

American bar, a trend that had also spread throughout the country, albeit complaints were frequent about both the quality and price of the drinks, particularly, it seems, in Glasgow.

FROM COCKTAILS TO COCAINE

When cocktails underwent a resurgence in the United Kingdom in the years following the First World War and Spanish Influenza, American barmen such as Harry Craddock sought sanctuary from Prohibition in London's bars and hotels even though they were not universally welcomed. In the summer of 1921, media mogul Alfred Harmsworth, proprietor of, among others, *Evening News*, *Daily Mail*, *The Times* and *Observer* launched a co-ordinated attack in his numerous titles on 'the insidious cocktail'. Medical authorities warned 'that a growing number of people do not content themselves with one or two, but drink four or five, or even as many as eight, before luncheon or dinner …'. Articles complained that 'the secrets of the cocktail mixer are more closely guarded than those of the chef', hinting at some underhand or sinister intent on the part of the mixologist. For women in particular, cocktails represented a downhill path to moral turpitude, with many media outlets taking the rather strong view that a habit of cocktails quickly led to a habit for something altogether much stronger; 'Cocaine evil among girls', 'Girl druggers', 'Cocaine girls', 'Cocaine victims' ran the headlines in Harmsworth's press as the anti-cocktail campaign continued. But for all of these and other dire warnings, London's cocktail craze continued unabated; in 1930 Johnnie Walker's Francis Redfern suggested to his colleagues on the Distillers Company Blending Committee 'that if we could convert the public to drinking whisky cocktails it might be a good thing'.

OLD-FASHIONED HOT TODDY

Rocks glass or tumbler

2 teaspoons dark unrefined sugar
60ml boiling water
50ml Scotch (preferably smoky)
7.5ml lemon juice

Garnish: lemon wedge

— Mix the sugar with 20ml of the boiling water in glass;
add the Scotch and lemon juice and remaining boiling
water and stir. Garnish with lemon wedge. Drink hot!

The idea of mixed whisky drinks, of whisky cocktails in Scotland, was as old as the hills. From the use of honey, herbs and fruit to flavour the earliest *aqua vitae* to the hot toddy, which when served cold, would become a whisky sour, or with the addition of lemon peel a whisky skin, the mixability of whisky had always been recognised. Early American cocktails tended to use domestic whiskies. Writing in 1923 George Saintsbury was uncharacteristically uncharitable in his assessment of them, writing that 'Walker's well known Canadian Club is the least unpalatable that I have tried'. They were made, he said, for 'drinking as liqueurs or cocktails … as such they are not repulsive'; in a sweet toddy they were 'not loathsome', with water they were 'nasty' and with soda 'worse'. The early American cocktails, as Dave Wondrich explains in *Imbibe!*, were simple combinations of sugar syrup, bitters and spirits – normally brandy, gin or whisky, possibly with a dash of curaçao. In New Orleans this would become a Sazerac, a slightly more sophisticated version with the addition of lump sugar and absinthe, elsewhere without the absinthe it was an Old Fashioned. In New York, with the arrival of sweet vermouth, it became the Manhattan. For some, of all of these the Manhattan is the closest thing to the perfect cocktail – though of course the choice of whisky, rye or bourbon, along with the brand of vermouth, makes a huge difference to the final drink. Don't be beguiled into thinking that cocktails are to be made from the cheapest components – just like cooking, the quality of the ingredients are key. Remember, it's all about balancing sweet and sour. And if you're experimenting and want to produce a smoky flavour in your Manhattan, then you'll obviously need to use a smoky whisky, most likely a Scotch. At that point, it could be argued that you're making a Rob Roy, one of the earliest Scotch whisky cocktails, apparently named not after the book, but a Broadway show from 1894. And yes, if you are experimenting with flavour and texture, then using a single malt whisky in your cocktail is fine, just like Alessandro Palazzi's smoky Lagavulin Negroni (or Boulevardier). Another showbusiness-inspired Scotch cocktail is the wonderful Blood and Sand, created from orange juice, cherry brandy, Scotch and sweet vermouth as a homage to Rudolph Valentino and the 1922 film of the same name. Other classic Scotch cocktails include the Rusty Nail (Scotch and Drambuie), the Bobby Burns ('one of the very best whisky cocktails' said Harry Craddock) and the dangerously dramatic burning Blue Blazer, which the great cocktailian Jerry Thomas claimed to have invented in the 1850s. As it would have been at the time, this requires a Scotch whisky at proof or ten under (that is to say between 51–57 per cent abv by today's measures) in order to deliver the desired incendiary effect.

ROB ROY

Coupe or rocks glass

50ml Scotch
30ml sweet vermouth
2 dashes Peychaud's bitters

Garnish: orange zest twist (discarded)
and maraschino cherry

— Stir all the ingredients with ice in a jug and strain into
a chilled glass.
— Squeeze the orange twist over the glass and discard.
— Garnish with the maraschino cherry.

Our whisky experts tended to gravitate to the sours, Manhattan and Old Fashioned when it came to cocktails, although Serge Valentin suggested the only mixing he did with his whisky was with water. Not all were conventional, Billy Abbott improvising 'a half and half Scotch whisky sour with a dash of liquorice vodka. Shake it up until foamy, strain into a glass and sprinkle on a smashed up Italian liquorice pastille. The liquorice fills any gaps, and gives it not only a nice sweetness, but also helps it get excellently frothy'. Richard Woodard confessed to enjoying a bottled cocktail from Hawksmoor in London during lockdown, the Fuller-Fat Old Fashioned, made using brown butter-infused bourbon ('my proverbial socks were blown across the room'). Becky Paskin opted for the Bobby Burns, 'possibly the most underrated Scotch cocktail. Equal parts Scotch and sweet vermouth with a few drops of Benedictine, it works best with a meaty, waxy whisky like Clynelish or Craigellachie'; Kurt Maitland chose the Vieux Carré, sort of similar but made with rye and cognac. Sukhinder Singh went for a variation of a modern classic, the Penicillin, with a drop of the aged Chartreuse VEP. Everyone was clear on the importance of ingredients: 'I love cocktails that retain the intensity of whisky even after other ingredients have been added,' said Isabel Graham-Yooll, 'I normally go for an Old Fashioned unless I can have a Boulevardier'. The most important advice to someone starting out on whisky cocktails? First, get yourself a recipe book and for all the multiplicity of volumes published on the subject you could do much worse than a copy of *The Savoy Cocktail Book*, originally published in 1930, but frequently reprinted and easily available. Or for a modern well-measured source of recipes get a copy of *Difford's Guide*. Buy some vermouth (sweet and dry) and some bitters, a shaker, a long spoon, a strainer, some nice rye whisky, some bourbon, a good Scotch blend, a smoky single malt and simply have fun. Don't listen to the killjoys – drinking whisky is all about having fun. Why else would you do it?

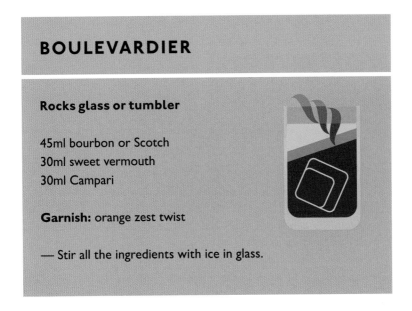

BOULEVARDIER

Rocks glass or tumbler

45ml bourbon or Scotch
30ml sweet vermouth
30ml Campari

Garnish: orange zest twist

— Stir all the ingredients with ice in glass.

WHISKY EXPERTS AND EXPERTISE

06

MILROY'S MALT WHISKY ALMANAC

CELLAR BOOK

FROM BURN TO BOTTL

THE WHISKY DISTILLERIES
OF THE
UNITED KINGDOM

ALT WHISKY COMPANION

'It is true, of course, that there are "cranks" who profess to know about whisky who can even undertake to instruct the most proficient member of our trade as to how he should conduct his business. Fortunately, these individuals are a minority but that they can and do make themselves troublesome at times, almost all of our trade knows by practical experience.'

— *Wine & Spirit Trade Record*, 8 April 1905

The world of whisky is a difficult place to navigate, particularly for those making their first tentative steps into an industry renowned for its ability to overcomplicate even the simplest parts of the process. From almost-impossible-to-pronounce distillery names, to the bewildering number of new releases and the increasingly arcane points of difference claimed by distillers and producers, it's not an easy place to be. While there are lots of regulations about how whisky is made, particularly in Scotland, there are no rules about how it should be drunk and enjoyed. Despite this, there is still lots of stuff you ought to know if you choose to enjoy the occasional 'dram'. That's why there are books like this. These days everyone wants to know a little more about what they consume. Questions, questions, questions. Where does it come from? How's it made? Who makes it? Is it kind to the environment? Is it really supposed to taste like this? Is it the right drink for me? Which one do I choose? How can a bottle of old whisky be worth over a million pounds? How much do I need to know to properly enjoy my glass of Scotch? Do you need to be an expert to enjoy whisky? Of course you don't. There are simple sensual pleasures to be had from a drink without having to learn a lexicon of obscure language or a textbook of technical detail. Will a little knowledge explain the difference between whiskies, help you decide what to buy and enhance your enjoyment? Probably; a little knowledge goes a long way. But you don't have to know everything; you can pick and choose what, if anything, you're interested in. That's the beauty of whisky – you can become your own expert with just a few facts to hand. After all, no one knows your own taste buds better than you do.

SO MANY EXPERTS

One thing the newcomer to the world of whisky will soon realise is that it is a place defined by knowledge, information and 'expertise'. The world of whisky, particularly unconstrained as it now is by the Internet, is like a sea awash with voices all shouting to be heard above the noise of the crashing waves. Some of this expertise is genuine, some is assumed and some is imaginary; 'so many experts, so little expertise' can at times feel like a very apt critique of the industry at large. So, when you venture online be sure to take care who you listen to. When you do find the real experts you'll know it; they tend not to be those who wear their expertise on their sleeves, but rather are considered, helpful and sometimes very generous with their time and advice. A lot of the competitive expertise that can haunt the Internet is rarely claimed by those who actually work or have worked in the real business of making whisky; maltsters, distillers, blenders and even, heaven forbid, marketing folk. With one or two notable exceptions these are among the most modest and unassuming people you are ever likely to meet, and meet them you can; at whisky shows, tastings and, if you're lucky, on distillery visits. They tend to be the sort of people who understand that the acquisition of knowledge and understanding is a continuous process, a sort of endless 'Scotch whisky journey' of enlightenment.

Two of the most knowledgeable people in the Scotch industry who certainly deserve the description of 'expert' might well have 'modesty' as their middle names, and both have been honoured by the Queen for their services to Scotch whisky. David Stewart MBE, who joined William Grant & Sons as a whisky stocks clerk in 1962 went on to become a blender and finally 'malt master' for the Balvenie. It took an apprenticeship of twelve years to develop the skills that would enable him to take over responsibility for William Grant's single malts and their blends. He was responsible for the development of the Glenfiddich Solera Reserve. As we've seen (see page 64), his pioneering work on cask finishes is much admired in the industry, particularly for the 21-year-old Balvenie PortWood finish, and also for the extension of finishing process to Grant's blends. However, ask anyone in the industry about David Stewart and they are most likely not to list his accomplishments first, but would start by saying 'he is such a lovely man'. Jim Beveridge OBE studied seed potatoes before joining the Distillers Company in 1979 to turn his attention to the science of the aromas and flavours of whisky. He spent years studying distillation and maturation, travelling around the distilleries and warehouses of Scotland, and spending countless hours with samples at his table to understand the intricacies of whisky making. In the process he developed a remarkable olfactory memory and understanding of the spirit and its behaviour for blending. This softly spoken and hugely cerebral man has been responsible for Diageo's Scotch whisky portfolio of single malts and blends, the largest in the world, since the early 1990s and in that time has been responsible for numerous innovations that have stemmed from his deep knowledge and understanding of whisky. Described by one leading drinks writer as 'a modest, self-effacing man, frankly unlike many

A lot of the competitive expertise that can haunt the Internet is rarely claimed by those who actually work or have worked in the real business of making whisky; maltsters, distillers, blenders and even, heaven forbid, marketing folk.

brand ambassadors,' Beveridge makes a lasting impression on anyone he meets. Both Stewart and Beveridge are true experts and masters of their craft, although you won't find either of them on Instagram.

A LITTLE TOO MUCH KNOWLEDGE CAN BE A DANGEROUS THING ...

Expertise also has something to do with connoisseurship, although the latter means not just the possession of knowledge, but the ability to discern, to discriminate and to judge. A connoisseur might also be called an aficionado, although this word is most likely to be used in a derisory or ironic sense today. Connoisseurship is intrinsically linked with notions of status, social standing and privilege; to be a connoisseur is to be elevated, or to elevate oneself to a position of superiority over others. Connoisseurship also implies wealth, not just material wealth but that precious commodity of leisure time to indulge in one's passion. Connoisseurship is also about possession of knowledge or expertise and about control. Connoisseurs are tastemakers, particularly in the field of comestibles; through their judgement and appraisal they define what others will aspire to appreciate and enjoy. Connoisseurs in any particular field, whether it be wine, coffee, cheese or whisky, develop and use a shared language, rich in specific meaning yet often deliberately obscure to outsiders, to define and assess and judge the merits of various items. They might sometimes also add scores or points as signifiers of degrees of quality. As we've seen, this is what happens in the process of writing tasting notes. Sadly in real life it is always too easy for aspiring connoisseurs in a particular field to learn and persuasively adopt the shared language in order to fool others about their real level of knowledge and expertise. So, without any form of

The world of whisky, particularly unconstrained as it now is by the Internet, is like a sea awash with voices all shouting to be heard above the noise of the crashing waves. Some of this expertise is genuine, some is assumed and some is imaginary; 'so many experts, so little expertise' can at times feel like a very apt critique of this 'Scotch whisky community'.

>

EVERYTHING YOU NEED TO KNOW ABOUT WHISKY

accreditation of whisky connoisseurship (there is no 'Master of Whisky' equivalent to a 'Master of Wine') you can never be quite sure who you're listening or talking to.

None of this should be taken as a criticism of expertise and connoisseurship – both are critical in legitimising a new category to those with the money and time to indulge in it. Both are essential if you want to transform the ordinary into the extraordinary, as has really happened with Scotch single malts and whisky more generally around the world during the past 20–30 years. Both provide reasons and rationale in the minds of producers, retailers and consumers for paying increased prices. They validate the desirability and value of limited and rare editions or releases, by providing apparently objective reasons to purchase. To some extent they underpin the market. And in the connected world of whisky enthusiasts, they provide leadership and role models for others. However, as the world of wine found out the hard way, experts and connoisseurs are not without their flaws, as leading authority Michael Broadbent demonstrated when his connoisseur's judgement was found to be sorely wanting in the case of Thomas Jefferson's supposed vintage French wines, or 'the billionaire's vinegar'. Acknowledged connoisseurship and expertise tends to promote vanity, and perhaps a little too much self-confidence, as those wealthy wine collectors who fell for Rudy Kurniawan's fake Domaine de la Romanée-Conti discovered to their cost.

THE DEVELOPMENT OF DISCERNMENT

Who were the first whisky experts; the original whisky connoisseurs? It makes sense to attribute some degree of expertise to the early whisky makers, possibly handed down from generations of farm distillers, or from the many published handbooks relating to distilling that appeared from the second half of the eighteenth century. Were the first connoisseurs those 'chief men of the isles' described by Martin Martin in his *A Description of the Western Islands of Scotland* in or around 1695, sitting in a circle and drinking from a communal vessel, until they all, one by one, collapsed and were carried to bed? And were these first connoisseurs drinking *usquebaugh*, or *trestarig*, three times distilled, 'strong and hot', or *usquebaugh-baul* 'which at first taste affects all the members of the body', two spoonfuls of which would prevent breathing and endanger life? As we've already seen, from around the middle of the eighteenth century, retailers of whisky began to develop a crude consumer language for Scotch whisky that was built around notions of discernment: whiskies were 'fine', 'very fine', and 'one-year-old superfine', with each being priced accordingly. Such gradations of quality and price were already well understood in the world of tea, which so many whisky retailers also dealt in. John MacCulloch, the famous nineteenth-century Scottish geologist who travelled widely and frequently in the Highlands, was clearly writing of discernment, if not connoisseurship, when he wrote in 1824 that 'the superior quality of the Highland whisky is acknowledged by all the learned …'. 'That of Arran,' he added with a wistful look to the past, 'in the olden days, was the Burgundy of all the vintages'. Clearly here was someone who rated his whisky with the precision that an oenophile might his or her finest wine. His expertise was such that he understood why this Highland whisky had been so good in the past; it was about the detail of the making, the quality of the malted barley and the quality of the wash that would eventually be distilled. And as discussed previously, some of these Highland distilleries and whisky-producing areas had reputations that went before them: 'there are some places' wrote the author of *The Hotel, Inn-keeper, Vintner and Spirit Dealer's Assistant* in 1825 'more famed for the goodness of their whisky than others, such as Glenlivet, Ferintosh, Campbeltown, Crieff etc.'. Retailers would advertise the availability of these makes in their windows to attract

a discerning clientele. The whisky with the highest reputation
was that which was smuggled from the small Highland stills into
the growing towns and cities of Scotland's central belt; every
nascent expert and connoisseur sought out this 'real mountain
dew' for its 'bouquet and pleasing flavour'.

There was, of course, no lack of familiarity with wine and
fortified wines or imported brandy in Scotland, although cost
confined it 'to the tables of the opulent, or to gratify the palate of
the luxurious'. George Saintsbury, who became a cult figure in the
world of oenophily with the publication of his *Notes on a Cellar-
Book* in 1920, 'never drank better claret or champagne' than he
did when he lived in Elgin, the capital of the distilling region of
Speyside in Morayshire. It would have been predominantly here
that the world of connoisseurship existed in the early nineteenth
century, when whisky was rarely seen outside of the Highlands,
rather than with the 'middling or inferior classes'. If the urban
middle class wanted to demonstrate expertise in drink then it was
in the preparation and consumption of rum punch. In Glasgow, a
rum dealer called Walter Graham, but known throughout the city
as 'the General', was considered to be the best judge of the quality
of rum punches. Whenever one was made in the presence of this
connoisseur the first glass was presented to him for his opinion,
if 'it wanted a little more of the lemon, rum, or sugar, the landlord
never failed to make the necessary additions and alterations, till
the beverage finally met the approbation of this distinguished
Gustatorius'. We have already seen that by the 1860s diners at
fine tables were wont to desert their fine wines in favour of whisky
toddy rather than rum punch, expertly made with blended whisky.
Many, with sufficient wealth to keep a good cellar, blended their
own whisky at home. 'It is not an uncommon circumstance,' wrote
Charles Tovey in 1860, 'to find in a gentleman's cellar a hogshead
or a half hogshead of whisky nearly always full ... when eight or
ten gallons is consumed, the cask is filled up with any whisky that
is particularly approved, and thus the spirit becomes well matured

and a perfect blend'. Men like Tovey, a bastion of the wine trade, lived in a world of expertise and connoisseurship, as did their upper-class customers with their well-stocked wine cellars. George Saintsbury had also kept a 'living cask' where he blended whiskies such as Clynelish, Glenlivet, Glen Grant, Talisker and Lagavulin, often secretly acquired from men like Tovey. Blended whisky, however, was on the march in terms of its reputation, quality and consumption by the 'middling' classes largely as a result of blending malt whiskies with grain. The expertise, the ritual and the (not inexpensive) paraphernalia involved in toddy making elevated the status of blended whisky and promoted a sense of discernment around its consumption.

WHISKY SNOBS

The people finding their way in this new world of whisky were like John Gourlay, a character in George Douglas Brown's gloomy novel *The House with the Green Shutters*, published in 1901. A student returned from the University of Edinburgh to his small home town in Ayrshire, Gourlay demonstrated his sophistication and discernment to his neighbours at the local bar, having been flattered with the comment that 'university men normally have a fine taste in spirits'. In George and Weedon Grossmith's *Diary of a Nobody*, which perfectly captures lower middle-class London life in the late nineteenth century, the aspiring actor Lupin Pooter and son of the fictional diarist, was keen to demonstrate his newly gained expertise in Scotch blends to his father, as were two family friends Cummings and Going, and the local wine merchant. Blended Scotch was a craze, and everyone wanted to have the expertise and knowledge to be a part of it, to be on the inside. Grudgingly connoisseurs of single malt whiskies in the trade acknowledged the inevitably of the changing times: 'it is all very well,' wrote the *Victualling Trades Review* in July 1897, 'for enthusiasts, who consult only their own personal likings, to say there is nothing like malt … but it is the millions of the middle class who have to be catered for, and not the few who can afford to drink malt whisky'. The new proprietary blends of malt and grain whisky were designed for relatively untrained palates, for the Mr and Mrs Pooters of this world who had not been given an education in the fine art of drinking. Blending not only democratised Scotch, it also democratised expertise and connoisseurship; it lowered the bar. Unlike single malts, blended Scotch was easier to acquire a taste for, and generally kinder to a moderately critical palate.

The old experts and connoisseurs like J A Nettleton and George Saintsbury mourned the decline in the availability and consumption of their treasured single malts, and were contemptuous of a new generation of middle-class whisky drinkers, who lacked their skills of discernment and knowledge. Nettleton refused to defer to the judgement of the man in the street and Saintsbury never cared for the blends. But they were yesterday's men, 'the Old School' who preferred the old-fashioned full peat flavour that most drinkers found so difficult. Moreover, significant long-term social and economic changes brought about by the First World War further embedded blended Scotch whisky as the people's choice. 'The gulf between the classes and the masses gradually becomes narrower,' wrote Ridley's *Wine and Spirit Circular* in 1920, 'and the whisky of today is as much the drink of the West End aristocracy as it is of the Billingsgate fish-carrier'. These old school backwoodsmen would find their flag-

Well-chosen books can be just as important to a collection as the whiskies themselves.

MILROY'S MALT WHISKY ALMANAC

CELLAR BOOK

FROM BURN TO BOTTLE

THE WHISKY DISTILLERIES OF THE UNITED KINGDOM

MALT WHISKY COMPANION

bearer in Aeneas MacDonald, whose polemic *Whisky* (some of it plagiarised from Nettleton) was an uncompromising reassertion of the supremacy of the traditional connoisseur, and a disdainful dismissal of the 'ordinary' drinker, who, with his whisky and soda, was incapable of ever penetrating the mysteries of *aqua vitae*. His book was intended for 'the earnest student of whisky', a handbook for the budding aficionado and a manual of whisky snobbery. He believed that the disappearance of whisky as a civilised pleasure from the connoisseur's table was symbolic of a general decline of taste in Scotland. As we've seen, he also linked the democratisation of Scotch with the idea of moral and national decline. He looked back and longed for an age when 'whisky still held its place in the cellars of the gentry and of men of letters, who selected it with as much care and knowledge as they gave to the stocking of their cellars with claret'.

'FINGS AIN'T WOT THEY USED T'BE!'

This yearning for a lost and better past, 'the good old days', is a pervasive and persistent part of the narrative of connoisseurship. The world of whisky is no exception and, as we shall see, a profound sense of a lost past is a major theme in some of the best of Scotch whisky literature. It's the Golden Age theory, itself almost as old as the hills, writ large. We've already seen that as early as 1824 John MacCulloch lamented the loss of the Arran whisky that had been available in the 'olden days'. In 1903 whisky merchant Adam Findlater could mourn the demise of 'rich old whisky with an enormous peaty flavour'. 'Nowadays,' he continued, 'a big fat whisky won't do at all'. In 1904 the *Wine & Spirit Trade Record* recalled the high quality of whisky once got from 'the old-fashioned golden Sherry casks', now long gone. Twenty years or so later, George Saintsbury similarly harked back to the days of toddy whiskies and the dark, sweet whiskies obtained from 'golden sherry or Madeira' casks. He despised the 'abominable tyranny' of the changes introduced during the First World War that lowered the standard bottling strength of whisky to 40 per cent abv and longed once more for 'the blissful times' of full-strength Scotch.

At least these Golden Agers had had direct experience of the times they yearned to return to. Today's have created a make-believe past which is carefully reconciled to their view of the present, a past that everything about whisky was better than it is today. That's not to say that whiskies from the past weren't good; some are quite exceptional, and very different from whiskies that you might taste today. You can find out yourself too; it's still possible to try some of them as a result of the growth of whisky auctions. Blends from the 1960s and 1970s, miniatures and full bottles, can be bought and tasted relatively cheaply, although malts from the period are scarce and costly because so few were produced. So, you can buy, try and make your own mind up.

Blending not only democratised Scotch, it also democratised expertise and connoisseurship; it lowered the bar. Unlike single malts, blended Scotch was easier to acquire a taste for, and generally kinder to a moderately critical palate.

But 'good' and 'different' do not necessarily add up to 'better'. As we've seen, the past hundred and fifty years have been nothing if not years of change in terms of how whisky is made and how whisky tastes. If you ask the question 'is the generality of whisky enjoyed around the world today better or worse than it was fifty or a hundred years ago?' then the answer has to be 'better'.

THE WHISKY RENAISSANCE

The new Scotch enthusiasts began to emerge at that critical point in the late 1950s and early 1960s when quotas and allocations were gradually removed from sales of whisky in the United Kingdom, and price restrictions, formerly imposed by the Scotch Whisky Association, abolished, setting the stage for entrepreneurs like Jack Milroy to flourish. This was the point at which, as we have seen, the single malt resurgence began. Academics, journalists, writers, legal and medical professionals appear to have made up the core of these early aficionados, although to be honest a photograph of a long queue outside Milroy's Soho shop in Christmas 1964, attracted no doubt by keen prices and the four malt whiskies they had on offer, looks more like a line of ne'er-do-wells outside an adult bookstore. Books were to be increasingly important in spreading the word, knowledge and expertise about Scotch, and developing an idea of connoisseurship. J M Robb, Sir Robin Bruce Lockhart and Ross Wilson led the way in the 1960s, followed by David Daiches and James Ross in the 1960s. Publishers David & Charles produced a new edition of Alfred Barnard's *The Whisky Distilleries of the United Kingdom* with a scholarly introduction in 1969. Even the normally reticent Scotch industry seemed to realise it needed to say something about itself, and in 1953 the Scotch Whisky Association published the first edition of its *Questions and Answers* booklet, still in print today. They also reprinted Hastie's

From Burn to Bottle in 1956. In 1962 the notoriously secretive Distillers Company published an illustrated booklet *The DCL & Scotch Whisky*, which would go into several reprints. The importance of the decision by William Grant to open a Visitor Centre at Glenfiddich in 1969 cannot be overstated; although others were slow to follow their move. As late as 1975, the DCL refused to see any benefit in the idea of opening distilleries to the public in terms of sales.

It was the acceleration of single malt availability and sales in the late 1980s that saw the arrival of the modern whisky connoisseur. This was particularly true of United Distillers' Classic Malts, which offered a simple route to consumers, from novitiate to expert in a tasting pack of six miniatures. For restaurants or bars with none or just one or two malts the mixed case of six different bottles was enough to turn them into a malt whisky specialist. The idea had first been developed in the last days of the DCL with Wallace Milroy acting as a consultant; the result, a collection known as the Malt Cellar, went on to sponsor Milroy's *Malt Whisky Almanac*, in the same way that the Classic Malts would produce a bespoke version of Michael Jackson's *Malt Whisky Companion*. Information was everything, and it soon became clear that the new connoisseur had a thirst for knowledge that matched, or even surpassed their thirst for whisky. And as with the whisky, when they demanded information, they wanted the real thing – not just romanticised marketing stories written by copywriters who knew little about their subject. If distillers and producers wouldn't provide it, then they would look for it from the increasing number of third-party experts and authorities, or they would go and find it themselves, or sometimes just make it up. This provoked some interesting internal tensions in larger companies where a Chinese wall traditionally separated sales and marketing functions and production – distillers and technical experts were reluctantly forced to open up their Pandora's box of secrets. That included opening up distilleries, and so visitor centres, or 'brand homes', popped up everywhere, with the training and scripts for guides becoming increasingly demanding. Out (for the most part) went stories of sea-lashed casks and seaweed or treasured water sources, in came distillery character, fermentation times and maturation mechanisms. And, of course, the more the information was supplied, the more was demanded. Whether from global consumer educational programmes like *The Friends of the Classic Malts*, at Distillery-Manager- or Brand-Ambassador-led consumer tastings, or from specialist retailers like Richard Joynson's Loch Fyne Whiskies with its irreverent *Scotch Whisky Review* or The Whisky Exchange, or at the new whisky shows that started to appear in Europe and the United States in the late 1990s and on the first dreadfully over-designed websites, content had become king. These new experts and connoisseurs drank up facts like fish.

It was the acceleration of single malt availability and sales in the late 1980s that saw the arrival of the modern whisky connoisseur, and with it an increased demand for information – not just the type written by copywriters in marketing departments, but the real thing. That included opening up distilleries, and so visitor centres, or 'brand homes', popped up everywhere, with the training and scripts for guides becoming increasingly demanding.

WHISKY EXPERTS GO DIGITAL

What no one could quite have anticipated was the impact that the development of the Internet would have on the growth of what some like to call 'the Scotch whisky community', a world of extreme fandom, of enthusiasts, self-styled experts, connoisseurs real and imagined, and influencers. The first whisky website, 'The Edinburgh Malt Whisky Tour' was set up by John Butler in 1994, an experiment which became in effect a pre-Wikipedia Scotch Whisky wiki, with information on distilleries and brands, history, production and, naturally, tasting notes gleaned from a variety of disparate sources. It was also a guide to the whisky clubs and societies that had started to spring up all over the world, and a gateway to the first 'community' space, the Karlsruhe Malts List, a Bulletin Board where like-minded fans could meet, discuss and, as soon became apparent, complain. A year later, Johannes van den Heuvel set up his Malt Madness website which became the rallying point for the Malt Maniacs, a small yet hugely influential 'international collective' of well-informed and highly opinionated connoisseurs who issued regular 'e-pistles' with all the authority of Moses handing down tablets of stone. They also began an annual awards programme to rival those sprouting up all over the drinks industry funded by magazines and others. One of their number, Serge Valentin, set up a website of regularly updated tasting notes in 2002, which remains one of the most important and frequently referenced sites for companies and consumers alike; although he dislikes the title, Valentin is certainly the Robert Parker of Scotch, with the power to make or break a new whisky in a few witty strokes of a keyboard. The Maniacs now have their own Facebook group (with almost 20,000 members), one of the many that deal with different aspects of whisky ranging from broken corks to spirit safe collectors, and all points in between.

Clearly many people who are part of these groups find them useful, informative and entertaining, rightly seeing them

No one could have anticipated the impact that the development of the Internet would have on the growth of what some like to call 'the Scotch whisky community', a world of extreme fandom, of enthusiasts, self-styled experts, connoisseurs real and imagined, and influencers.

∧

as a way of sharing their views with fellow enthusiasts and even making new friends. Some do enjoy seeing pictures posted there or on Instagram of bottles, shelves of bottles and often rooms full of bottles, but beware the social media curse of photographs of 'influencers' living the high life at someone else's expense, plugging their latest freebies. As everyone knows, there's a lot of braggadocio and sometimes bullying on social media and sadly the world of whisky is no exception. There is also a surprising amount of outrage, which seems odd given that whisky is supposed to be about having fun. And although this is only a very small part of the whisky world, what they say might lead you to think that something important seems to have gone missing. In this over-informed world where everything is about the rational, the functional and facts, it's a shame that a few have lost sight of the aesthetic, romance and emotion of whisky. In the true meaning of the word 'connoisseur' there resides an ability to recognise and rejoice in exquisiteness, to relish a thing of beauty for what it is, to rejoice in the craft that has produced such a thing of wonder, of uniqueness, wrought from such simplicity. This is the genuine spirit of whisky connoisseurship.

So if you're new to whisky, or you're new to wanting to find out about more about whisky, where best to start? Bernhard Schäfer, author and judge at many international drinks competitions, probably summed up the thoughts of all of our industry insiders: 'drink and repeat! Visit distilleries, read books, do not listen to YouTubers and that ilk!' 'Taste, taste, taste again,' said Dave Broom, 'go to whisky shows. Ask why. Listen to the answers. Taste more.' 'There are so many things you can learn about whisky, but at its core, the flavour, aroma and texture of the spirit in the bottle is what it's all about,' said The Whisky Exchange ambassador and writer Billy Abbott, 'and is from where all other knowledge flows. Without tasting and building your knowledge of the possibility of flavour it's hard to learn more.' Make it a social activity, 'Learn with friends,' said collector and bar owner Emanuel Dron and 'taste as many as you can.' 'Join a club, go to shows, read books but be very selective about all the advice you may be given from people who believe they are more experienced. Whisky is a very personal thing,' said *Malt Whisky Yearbook*'s Ingvar Ronde. There are so many whisky clubs, normally friendly groups of like-minded people who just want to learn and share their enthusiasm for whisky with others; you should try and find one. 'Ask questions,' said Becky Paskin; 'read, taste, visit and talk to people who work behind the scenes,' said Davin de Kergommeaux; 'visit distilleries and talk to management and workers. Better yet, to former management and former workers,' added Whiskyfun's Serge

In the true meaning of the word 'connoisseur' there resides an ability to recognise and rejoice in exquisiteness, to relish a thing of beauty for what it is, to rejoice in the craft that has produced such a thing of wonder, of uniqueness, wrought from such simplicity. This is the genuine spirit of whisky connoisseurship.

Valentin. 'I have learned most,' said whisky auction director Isabel Graham-Yooll, 'from listening to the experiences of long-serving industry professionals.' 'Go to tastings,' said author and broadcaster Rachel McCormack, 'you get the fun and the education and the atmosphere at the same time.' Perhaps not surprisingly, Sukhinder Singh said 'The Whisky Show, of course. Any whisky fair where you can try lots of different whiskies, talk to the people that made them and enjoy the company of like-minded individuals.' Although no one questioned the importance of reading books, the clear consensus here was that learning about whisky, starting that 'whisky journey' towards expertise was more of an experiential process than simply the accumulation of facts and figures. It was, as Billy Abbott said, about 'practice' – just like learning to play the guitar or ride a bike. It was about being inquisitive, about trying to have the right conversations with the right people, and seeing and smelling the making of whisky (wherever you may be in the world) at first hand. There's almost something metaphysical about this, in submitting yourself to a greater spirit, to achieve a higher state of being. Something approaching connoisseurship. And if you do go online? There was much affection for the Scotchwhisky.com website, still available but no longer updated, and predictably for Serge Valentin's witty Whiskyfun. As for Valentin's opinion? 'Malt Maniacs as it was fifteen years ago, before many got too tired or too old. Or too grumpy. Or their doctors told them to stop.'

WHISKY COLLECTORS AND COLLECTING

07

'Every passion borders on chaos, but the collector's passion borders on the chaos of memories.'

— Walter Benjamin, *Unpacking My Library*, 1931

Everyone collects something, right? Don't shake your head and tell me you don't. Just think about all that stuff you've got. What about those beer mats, carefully liberated from student bars and pubs and now discarded in a cupboard? And don't you remember you told me you once bought some in an antique shop in Rye because they looked unusual and you'd never seen them before? And the gig tickets; the Astoria, the Mean Fiddler, Led Zeppelin at the O2, Glastonbury 2005 with Coldplay and Kasabian, and all those that your Auntie Lala gave you from the 1970s. Didn't you sort the whole lot out by date? And the spoons; I know you've been buying spoons on the Internet and at antique fairs, and swapping them with people you've met there. I bet you've got drawers full of spoons in your kitchen and you never allow anyone to use them. I suppose you never play any of those vinyl albums you've been keeping for all these years; are you still going to all those vintage vinyl websites and that store in Brick Lane in search of that Dylan bootleg album that you could never get your hands on? What about the Panini 2018 World Cup football cards – did you ever get the full set? Don't you have a few bottles of whisky too? The good ones you've bought at distilleries in Scotland and never opened. The ones you get given every Christmas by the people who know you like something unusual. You do? I knew it. A whisky collection! Thirty-eight bottles! And you've got photographs of them all on your phone. Oh …

IT'S ALL IN THE MIND ...

There's something about whisky and collecting. From two bottles to 2,000, most whisky drinkers have a collection of sorts, even those who refuse to use the 'C' word. It normally starts as a couple of bottles, perhaps some unwanted gifts. Bottles opened; bottles drunk. But some bottles, *the special ones*, get put to the back of the cupboard. Saved for a special occasion that never arrives. They're joined by more. You can't drink them all ... can you? Or you could buy two bottles, drink one and save the other. Then you decide you're going to specialise; just whiskies from one area or one distillery, just blends produced by one brand. Before you know it there's a bookcase full of bottles. You might stop there, but for some collecting becomes an obsession, a quest in search of the Holy Grail of whiskies, whatever that might be. A bottle of the elusive Malt Mill perhaps? Rooms full of bottles, storage pods full of bottles. Too many bottles to put on display. Collections can be organic. Bottles bought and sold or bottles swapped. They can also be speculations: a decent investment at a time when normal interest rates return next to nothing. Think of this: a bottle of 22-year-old single malt from Brora, a closed distillery on Scotland's exposed north-east coast, was released in 1995 and sold for around £40. Today if you can find one, it might cost you in the region of £10,000. Not a bad return over twenty-five years or so. Is a speculator a collector? Not really, not if they're the sort that want to buy and sell bottles like commodities. But a collection can be a speculation, accruing value over time just as a first growth Bordeaux in a wine cellar might. Can you open bottles in your collection? Not really. You can read books in your book collection (although some collectors consider it a badge of honour never to have read any of their books) and you can play records in your record collection, but you can't drink whisky in your whisky collection. Some get over this awkward difficulty by having a 'drinking collection' and a 'keeping collection'. Finally, you should know that it's not just bottles that people collect.

You may (or may not) be surprised to know that Freud believed that the urge to collect was linked back to anal eroticism and infant experiences – it was, he said, all about potties and poo. Others have argued that the drive to collect is a way of dealing with early childhood neurosis around the fear of abandonment; a collection offers security and safety, just as a child's toys might. It can also be a substitute for real relationships with real people. A tendency towards exhibitionism and the need for approval, all derived from these childhood fears and traumas, might also be factors at play. Collecting is certainly about control; it's about organising and imposing order and coherence on a group of pieces or things – that's what differs collecting from simply hoarding or accumulating. It's also about the specialness of the objects being collected, which, it has been suggested, almost in the act of collection transfer from the mundane to the 'sacred'. We all define ourselves by the material objects we possess; they express our status, our wealth and our self-image or how we want to be seen by others. Having a collection can be a supercharged version of this. Collecting is certainly a state of mind; it's about developing strategies and sometimes deceptions in order to acquire new items, it's about the thrill of the chase (neurologists have determined that it is the pleasure that derives from the anticipation of an acquisition), the fear of failure, and the deep and addictive sense of satisfaction that comes from a successful acquisition. It's hardly surprising that psychologists, cultural historians and social scientists find it such a fertile territory for research. However, if you want to read one thing about collecting, about the unrestrained *delight* in collecting (whatever childhood anxieties it may or may not be derived from), written in 1931 by an unashamed collector, then get hold of a very short essay by German philosopher Walter Benjamin, called 'Unpacking My Library'. It's not only short, but beautifully written.

MEET THE COLLECTORS

Claive Vidiz is a Brazilian who began collecting Scotch whisky in the 1970s; 'I didn't choose to start collecting Scotch whisky – I was chosen,' he said in a recent interview. Overseas business travel allowed him to pick up occasional bottles for enjoyment, but it was the gift of six bottles of malt whisky from Islay that made him take to the task of collecting seriously – that was when he was chosen. With an impressive network of contacts, many in the Scotch business, he was able to build up a remarkable collection of over 3,000 bottles, housed in a purpose-built room in his garden. In 2006, with Vidiz concerned at what the future might hold for his collection, Johnnie Walker owner Diageo agreed to buy it, and a few years later it went on public display at the Scotch Whisky Experience in Edinburgh where it is now the crown jewel of a visitor's tour. The sheer profusion of bottles on display is almost overwhelming. There are some very aged pieces, like a Buchanan's blend from 1897, but the majority represent the whiskies most commonly available in Latin America in the last quarter of the twentieth century. So, as one would expect, the collection is dominated by blended Scotches. Asked by an interviewer what it meant to him Vidiz said it was about remembrance, or as Walter Benjamin said of his book collection, that it was 'a spring tide of memories'. Another extensive collection which is also on display is the Valentino Zagatti collection. Born in Italy, Zagatti lost his eyesight as a boy after stepping on a landmine

> Collecting is certainly a state of mind; it's about developing strategies and sometimes deceptions in order to acquire new items, it's about the thrill of the chase.

in 1945. He became an accomplished accordion player, but in 1960 decided he would begin a collection of bottles of spirits, purchased with money he had been spending on cigarettes. The number of bottles soon multiplied and in the late 1960s he decided to focus on Scotch single malts, which at that point were becoming popular, and more easily available in Italy. The first bottle was an Aberlour acquired on Christmas Day 1966. Each new acquisition was entered into a braille catalogue and although sightless this collector could identify bottles by touch. The oldest bottle in the collection dates from 1843; over twenty of the whiskies were distilled in the nineteenth century. A quarter of the 3,000-plus bottles is from just three distilleries that were among the most popular in Italy in the 1970s and 1980s, Glenfarclas, Macallan and Glen Grant. Eventually as the collection outgrew his home, Zagatti sold it to a group of Dutch investors, and in 2015 it was shipped to the Netherlands where it can now be viewed in a purpose-built display at the premises of Scotch Whisky International at Sassenheim. The collection, which has been detailed in a five-volume published catalogue by Hans and Becky Offringa, was reportedly valued at €4.5 million.

One of the largest collections of whisky in the world is owned by Sukhinder Singh, co-founder of The Whisky Exchange. A reformed stamp collector, Singh began collecting whisky miniatures in the early 1980s and bought the first full-sized bottle for his collection in 1988, a malt whisky from the long-closed Kirkliston distillery near Edinburgh. It was acquired 'with a lot of persuasion' on a trip to Scotland to buy more miniatures from another collector. The collection now comprises 7,000 bottles of whisky, of which 5,500 are on display. The remaining 1,500, some duplicates, are what he calls 'special drinking whiskies'. It was Singh's original intention to collect one bottle from each distillery in Scotland, the oldest he could find, but as he confessed with a touch of understatement 'things got a little out of control, actually very out of control'. As he explained, 'the 1990s was an amazing time as a drinker, there were so many amazing whiskies available which were distilled in the 1960s and 1970s especially from independent bottlers, and I have many of these.' He collects with the eye of a connoisseur; the quality of the whisky, he argues, is the most important factor in planning a purchase, eventually more so than the age of the bottle or perceived rarity. 'I focus on historic bottles and bottlings where I find the whisky to be very special for my personal drinking. I have around fifty old bottles of single malts bottled pre-1940 and many one-off examples where I do not know of any others in collections. Out of the 7,000 whiskies, less than 5 per cent are recent bottlings from the last fifteen years.' Is there a favourite whisky in his collection? The Kirkliston has a special place in Singh's heart, as does a 1911 bottling of a 30-year-old Lagavulin by distillery owners Mackie & Co. He was in a bidding war for this one, having lost out on a similar bottle a few years earlier. This time he was successful, 'I was the happiest person ever,' and flew to Seattle to collect the bottle and hand carry it back to London: 'how could I trust anyone to pack and ship something so special to me?'

While the pace at which his collection grows has possibly slowed down a little, there is no sign of it stopping. 'I thought I would stop finding old bottles,' said Singh, but the increasing awareness of the value of old and rare whiskies as a result of increased interest and media coverage meant that people with old bottles tucked away in their homes began to take them to the market. 'I started discovering bottles that I did not know even existed, and the last ten years has actually been busy and expensive for me. Where I could buy bottles for a few hundred pounds I now have to spend a few thousand instead.' Nor is there any sign that the collecting will ever stop. Singh is no completist and there's no obvious end in sight, and there are still some 'unicorns' that he's searching for. These include a Dalaruan 1894, from a long-closed Campbeltown distillery, half a dozen bottles of which slipped through his hands a few years ago and ended up in the United States; a Highland Park 1941 which he's trying to persuade a friend to sell him and a bottle of Bowmore Sherriff's whisky from the late 1800s. 'I am still enthusiastic as ever and I might not be chasing bottles as much as I did in the early years, but somehow they find their way to me … at a price.' There's a purpose to his collection, well actually two purposes. 'I am very interested in the history of the Scotch whisky industry in particular and the collection tells this story'; Singh is rightly proud of this, and sees it as a life's work. But there's pleasure to be had from it too: 'I have been fortunate to have tried so many old whiskies and now understand what to expect when opening an old bottle. It is quite a special experience that must be shared with like-minded friends. With each bottle I buy the historic element is there but I am also always intrigued by what the whisky will be like.' Just one other thing about collectors like Sukhinder Singh; there's rarely only one collection. 'I also collect bottles from historic brands of other spirits including cognac, rum, gins, liqueurs,' he confessed: 'my Chartreuse collection is very special for me. I fell in love with this monastic liqueur in the late 1990s, today I have around a hundred old bottles including some from the mid-1800s.'

Any seasoned whisky collector will tell you that the journey of collecting can be a little addictive, and that it's all too easy for things to get a bit out of hand. Choosing a specific theme or subject for your collection will help keep it in order.

'HELP! I WANT TO START A COLLECTION ...'

So, if you're interested in starting a collection you might be asking 'where do I begin?' Singh insists it's best to buy what you like to drink, that always leaves you with a very clear exit strategy should the bottom fall out of the market. He also advises finding a theme; choose an area, or a specific distillery, or a brand, or a finite series like the Rare Malts, which will give you focus, particularly if you're on a limited budget. You might also want to try and find a theme that's unusual. Choosing Macallan, probably the most collected whisky in the world, would probably not be a good place to start. Picking Mortlach, or possibly a new distillery like Daftmill or Nc'nean, might be. Isabel Graham-Yooll, Whisky.Auction Director also offers some sage advice: 'have a think about why you want to collect whisky at all. Some questions you might ask yourself are: do you want to collect bottles that will gain in value? Are you planning on selling your whiskies or do you want to build up a collection of bottles to open later in life? Do you want your beautiful bottles on display to look at?' Thinking about the sort of collection you want, she added 'will help you build a better and more rounded collection from the moment you start'. Getting information is also critical; read, research, use websites and bulletin boards, sign up for mailshots from the retailers and producers you are interested in and get to know the people who run your local whisky specialist, if you're lucky enough to have one. You need to navigate through primary and secondary markets that have become increasingly crowded with 'collectibles'. Long gone are the innocent days when 'coach party collectors' would bring back the odd miniature from a trip to the Highlands with Happiways Holidays to join the others at the back of the drinks cabinet. Or when whisky collecting was all about the annual Bell's ceramic decanters and their special editions to celebrate largely royal events. Slowly whisky producers have begun to understand the power of the limited edition and the value of the special release, very much led by brands like Macallan, and this in turn has driven activity on the secondary market. Some of these collectible offerings are of truly astonishing whiskies of great age and rarity; others resemble rather more the anniversary plates and figurines you might see advertised on the back pages of the *Mail on Sunday*. As Graham-Yooll cautions: 'limited editions, numbered bottles and single-cask bottlings are intuitively attractive because they are finite. New shiny limited releases in their stunning presentation boxes may look like a good bet but will they stand the test of time?'

Bell's ceramic decanters, which were often released to celebrate important royal events, are a valuable relic of the old days of whisky collecting.

∧

Just remember that there are other people out there trying to find exactly the same bottles as you, and some of them have had a head start. Jon Beach, who runs the Fiddlers pub on the shore of Loch Ness, has been collecting Port Ellen since the 1990s, principally motivated by an interest in whisky and the fact that his mother was called Ellen. He describes himself as 'the world's worst Port Ellen collector' having accumulated over a hundred empty Port Ellen bottles in the process of assembling his 'modest' collection. Beach, it can be said, is a collector of taste as much as he is a collector of bottles. He is haunted by a comment from a friend about collecting Port Ellen, 'the first five hundred are easy to get hold of but the last six are impossible to find'. Marcel van Gils, a retired Dutch dentist, began collecting Laphroaig after visiting the distillery in 1994; he had a group of friends who were all collectors but none went for Laphroaig, so he did. He's written two books about the distillery and has a website for his collection, much of which he's now sold. He laments the expense and difficulty of starting a collection these days. Swiss accountant and collector Patrick de Schulthess has a collection that focuses on whiskies from Strathisla distillery in Keith on Speyside, although his purchases are far broader, including a bottle of 12-year-old Port Ellen bottled in 1980 to mark a visit to the maltings at Port Ellen by Queen Elizabeth II. This much sought-after bottle (it's

Jon Beach, who runs the Fiddlers pub on the shore of Loch Ness, has been collecting Port Ellen since the 1990s, principally motivated by an interest in whisky and the fact that his mother was called Ellen. He describes himself as 'the world's worst Port Ellen collector' having accumulated over a hundred empty Port Ellen bottles in the process of assembling his 'modest' collection.

another unicorn, the last one to be auctioned in 2021 reached £72,000) was opened in very distinguished company on a visit to Islay in 2015, to much acclaim – Whiskyfun's Serge Valentin scored it at 99 points. Collecting, says de Schulthess, has 'affected my life in different ways. It has obviously made me poorer, but also happier.' Like van Gils he also thinks he was lucky to start collecting in the 1990s when 'a lot of bottles were available at very low prices'. If you want to meet these people or see what they're like in action then a visit to The Whisky Exchange Old and Rare Whisky Show, or the fantastically crazy Limburg Whisky Festival is highly recommended. Otherwise, you are most likely to come up against them at whisky auctions.

GOING, GOING ...GONE

Up until around ten years ago whisky auctions were confined for the most part to occasional special wine and spirits or whisky-specific events at the Glasgow premises of smart auctioneers like Christie's or Phillips or to local provincial auction houses. From the late 1990s eBay had offered an alternative outlet for sale of collectable spirits but started banning this practice in 2012. In 2011 one of the first specialist online sites, Scotch Whisky Auctions, began operating out of Glasgow and since then over twelve have started based in the UK, with others in Europe and North America. A number of factors have contributed to the growth in interest in whisky to allow the secondary market to develop in this way: the wine market, which witnessed exponential growth after the financial crash of 2007 had peaked in 2011, and both wine traders and investors were looking for alternative investments at a time when interest rates were falling rapidly. There was a surge in interest in rare whiskies around the same time from consumers sparked by the continuing activities of brands like the Macallan, and things like the Diageo Special

Releases programme that brought these collectible whiskies to a much broader audience, both consumers and in the media. From the United States and Japan collectible whiskies like Pappy Van Winkle and Chichibu were also starting to sell at heady prices, with demand far outstripping supply. Consumers sometimes seemed to know the value of these whiskies better than the producers, and with brands like Port Ellen being sold for three or four times the retail price within days of release, enthusiasts were seeking platforms where they could buy, but more importantly sell, quickly and safely. Although there were well-established specialist online businesses, some of which handled rare whiskies (the 'exchange' part of The Whisky Exchange had always been intended as a place where enthusiasts could buy and sell) retailers in general had been slow to see the opportunity presented by the auction business model. As prices for rare bottlings continued to rise during the second decade of the twenty-first century, as more and more producers began to feed the market's appetite for 'special' bottlings and as more and more consumers were being told by the media that whiskies represented a sound investment, so the argument for online platforms became more compelling.

These developments provoked howls of outrage from some corners of the whisky world, where strong voices claimed the moral high ground and denounced speculators and investors for somehow defiling the culture of whisky by seeking to make a profit out of it. 'Flippers', those who bought special releases only to sell them on immediately through the auction sites were condemned as the lowest and most reviled form of whisky life. The good, the bad and the ugly fought it out on the battlefield of social media; some, like forgotten soldiers on Pacific islands, are still fighting the war. Graham-Yooll took a measured and sanguine view of this: 'from comments on social media there appears to be a great tribal divide between whisky drinkers, collectors, speculators and investors. However, the reality is far more interesting because the truth is that most whisky enthusiasts are to some degree

In 2011 one of the first specialist online sites, Scotch Whisky Auctions, began operating out of Glasgow and since then over twelve have started based in the UK, with others in Europe and North America.

∨

a combination of all these things. It's difficult to become a speculator if you don't have a collection to draw from and there are few collectors who don't enjoy the taste of whisky.' Graham-Yooll's auction services a global client base, some with 'extensive collections', but, she argues, bargains are always to be had: 'our auction is accessible to bargain hunters, cocktail bar staff, canny bar and restaurant buyers, international traders, traditional retailers and anyone just looking out for an interesting bottle that they wouldn't otherwise get the opportunity to taste.' For the record, although Whisky.Auction attracts buyers of all ages (over legal drinking age, of course) the most 'visible whisky enthusiasts are male and between 30–55 years old'.

LOOKS LIKE WHISKY, TASTES LIKE WHISKY ...

Things that some buyers are concerned about when they bid on older bottles of whisky at auctions are their provenance and also drinkability. Most auction houses go to great lengths to ensure that they are selling genuine bottles but it has to be acknowledged that there is a residual problem with counterfeit that affects both old or 'antique' bottles and more recent products. Just to be clear, the issue of counterfeit in spirits is not new, indeed, it's almost as old as the hills. By the last quarter of the nineteenth century, many brands of international repute, cognacs, whiskies, wines and liqueurs were subject to the most elaborate faking operations. Used bottles were collected on an industrial scale, and sometimes new bottles specially made to the moulds of the originals, and fake labels, corks and closures of the very highest quality applied, the bottles being filled with inferior liquids. Another common practice was 'substitution', refilling bottles, more often than not in pubs or bars. There were few geographies that were free from this fakery.

Brand owners and law enforcement agencies have been fighting this crime for well over a hundred years with the brands investing substantial sums in developing preventative measures. These are after all high-value luxury goods, where the profits to be made from forged products are substantial. Graham-Yooll acknowledged the long-standing existence of the problem: 'it's particularly frustrating for us when we see well-known, well-publicised fake rarities still circulating in the market. There are bottles that were identified as fakes decades ago that still hold pride of place in collections of unsuspecting whisky enthusiasts.' She also explained some of the measures taken to counter it: 'we are fortunate to have the most experienced team of whisky experts within our auction team, and they inspect every single bottle that is submitted to us. Sadly, we do regularly discover counterfeits that have slipped into the market but we have had some successes at removing bottles (as well as the criminals responsible) from the market. We have seen old and new bottles that have been faked.' Buy only from trusted sources, find out as much as you can about what you think you are buying (*Collecting Scotch Whisky: An Illustrated Encyclopaedia* by Emmanuel Dron is a very useful, if somewhat expensive, tool) and don't hesitate to complain if you think you've been sold a fake.

If you do get the bottle you wanted, and let's assume it's an old bottle of the White Horse blend from the 1960s, can you drink it? What should you expect? In theory, the answer would always be 'yes', as a spirit at 40 per cent abv or more shouldn't deteriorate in a sealed bottle. The seal, the closure, is the weakest link in the package. Up until the early twentieth century the majority of bottles were sealed using a driven cork, like many wines still are today. Cork stoppers, pioneered in whisky by William Teacher, were introduced in 1913, and screw caps, an innovation from White Horse, in 1925. Around the same time the Distillers Company bought an exclusive patent for a 'Kork 'n' Seal' closure, a closeable metal cap with an internal seal of an aluminium disc backed with cork, which was used on the majority of their brands until the 1960s. White Horse also used melamine screw tops with a similar aluminium and cork seal. A number of things could have happened to the whisky. It could be affected by cork taint just like a wine might be. The closure might have been damaged through poor storage or in transit, or the seal corrupted, leading to the whisky being contaminated. So, you need to open your old bottle with care and taste cautiously; if it's an old cork closure you'll need to be particularly careful about how you open it. If the liquid has been compromised you'll probably be able to tell quite quickly. There can be an extremely pungent vegetative aroma, a bit like boiled rotten cabbage, which is a good sign that something's not right. Give the whisky a bit of time to see if this dissipates. Also have a look at the liquid in the bottle before you start. If it's full of flock or other sediments, you might want to leave it sealed. If you've finally managed to pour some into a glass, then what's it supposed to taste like? Apart from the obvious 'whisky', we don't really know. These White Horse blends tend to be quite rich, there is a distinct flavour that comes from the use of paxarette (the sherry concentrate used to treat the casks) and they're slightly smoky, although not as smoky as one might expect. The problem is that there are no perfect time-capsule 'standard' samples of whiskies from the 1960s, or for that matter the 1940s, 1920s or 1900s against which you can judge these accidental survivors. Nor, as we have seen, are there any tasting notes to guide us. What we do know is that whisky does not mature in the bottle – the maturation processes of Scotch or any other style are confined to the wood – so in theory it should be exactly as it was when it went into the bottle. What we also know is that there have been numerous changes in production regimes and plants since the 1960s which might cause our whisky in the glass to taste different from today's. There is a strongly held belief by some connoisseurs that whiskies are subjected to 'old bottle effect' – that something changes in the character of the whisky over time in glass, some sort of oxidisation, that leads to specific and recognisable aromas and tastes. Some people have suggested component parts of a blend might disaggregate over time, also leading to changes in character. There's no science to support any of these views, but as is typical of whisky, they provoke endless debate and speculation. A final observation, in the author's experience White Horse blends from the 1960s taste almost uniformly delightful and delicious, and have a particularly wonderful mouthfeel.

CAVEAT EMPTOR ...

Why buy bottles for your collection, or for your investment, when you could buy a cask? What could be better than owning your own 250 litres of Scotch maturing slowly in some dusty warehouse, waiting to be bottled to mark a coming of age or a retirement? Over the past few years, the direct sale of casks to consumers by distillers and by brokers has exploded, and there are more companies promising investment advice on casks and whisky than there are card sharks playing find the lady on Westminster Bridge. Owning a cask can be fun, but it's fraught with risks. When you buy a cask you're only buying the whisky, and possibly (although not always) the wood. There are still significant costs for duty and packaging to be paid before you can bottle it. If you buy from a distillery – and many new distilleries today are desperate to sell casks as a way of generating income in advance of being able to sell any whisky in the bottle – they will normally impose certain conditions in their contract of sale that will restrict what you can and can't do with the cask after a specified maturation period. It may be that the distiller is the only person who can bottle it for you, using their preferred label, it may be that you are not able to sell the cask to anyone other than selling it back to the distiller. So check the paperwork. Also check the price. Even among these new distilleries there is a huge and totally inexplicable disparity in the price casks are offered at, with Islay commanding a rather cynical premium. And don't think you are getting a bargain. You will be paying far more than the trade price for the same cask. And that will be even more so if you buy a mature cask from a broker, which might still be subject to contractual constraints imposed on earlier owners. And if you're investing, that is to say putting your money into a business that claims to be buying casks on your behalf from which you will profit as their value appreciates, then be very careful indeed.

Selling casks that don't exist, or that you don't actually own, or getting people to invest in whisky that doesn't exist, is one of the oldest whisky scams in the book. In 1878, John Anderson of Talisker Distillery on the Isle of Skye, found himself in embarrassed circumstances after he set about selling casks of whisky to customers that had not been filled and bonded. He was eventually imprisoned for the offence. The Pattison Brothers of Leith, also imprisoned for their transgressions, sold the same casks of whisky to two different customers. Nearer the present time, consumers have been defrauded of tens of millions of pounds by bogus whisky investment schemes that flourished in the 1990s. Whisky is an unregulated investment. There is no control or oversight in the United Kingdom on companies promising huge returns to potential customers. Neither the Financial Services Authority nor the Scotch Whisky Association have any authority over, or oversight of these businesses with their slick websites, investment guides and 'influencer' endorsements. The phrase 'buyer beware' has never been more appropriate. If you want to have fun with a cask, buy one at a reasonable price from a distillery, go and visit it a few times, and then enjoy drinking it with your friends and family when it's ready. Whisky.Auction director Graham-Yooll, who occasionally sells casks alongside bottles, has some words of warning: 'the picture is complicated. Owning a cask and waiting for it to mature is potentially a wonderfully enjoyable hobby and it might even be profitable. On the other hand, it might not, and sadly cask-selling is not regulated so there's not much you can do to protect yourself from overenthusiastic sellers.'

Over the past few years the direct sale of casks to consumers by distillers and brokers has exploded, and there are more and more companies offering investment advice, many promising unlikely returns on casks. Knowing who to trust is often the trickiest part of the process.

>

EVERYTHING YOU NEED TO KNOW ABOUT WHISKY

IF IT MOVES, COLLECT IT ...

If you don't want to fill your house with bottles and you're rightly sceptical about owning a cask, then don't worry, whisky still has something to offer to the potential collector. From some point in or around the last quarter of the nineteenth century as the huge growth in sales of blended Scotch around the world combined with the emergence of a new science of advertising and promotion, there was an explosion in the production of printed publicity materials and what we call today 'point of sale', some of it, it has to be said, of remarkably high quality compared to the plastic ice-buckets of today. There was almost nothing that the owners of proprietary brands would not put their names on, everything was an opportunity to put your brand before consumers. From coat hangers to penknives, glasses, ashtrays, water jugs, figurines, decanters, wallets, cigarette cases, diaries, the list is endless. There is a vibrant memorabilia market both in Europe and the United States with regular collectors' fairs and online groups. Then there is also the printed publicity materials, from advertising postcards to Pattison's cycling maps of the United Kingdom (highly sought after). 'As a rule of thumb,' says Graham-Yooll, 'the most important thing is if the whisky brand is popular then the branded memorabilia will be too. Often it is the popularity of the brand rather than the usefulness of the item itself that affects its auction value.' Probably the largest collection of material of this sort is the Robert Opie Collection, which covers not just whisky, but focuses on the packaging and related memorabilia of consumer goods in nineteenth- and twentieth-century Britain. It's now housed in the Museum of Brands in West London and is well worth a visit for anyone interested in the field.

Housed just outside Edinburgh, what is known as the 'Scotch Whisky Archive' is one of the largest collections of printed and manuscript ephemera relating to Scotch whisky in the world. It's been thirty years in the making and comprises thousands of items of principally printed or manuscript, although the collection began with a passing interest in modern whisky decanters, which somehow led to distillery and advertising postcards, which then led on to the archive. They've got everything from old distillery postcards, old invoices and billheads, bottle labels, and old brochures and trade magazines. As if this wasn't enough, there are also several 'ancillary collections'. It is the most remarkable Aladdin's cave of stuff, not catalogued, but sorted into broad categories 'so that I can normally find an item I'm looking for relatively quickly' says the owner. This private collection is used by brands, antiquarians and publishers and may well end up being cared for by a major Scottish institution. It's still a work in progress, put together by a Lagavulin-loving collector and his wife, who started with bubblegum cards when he was a child and is still driven by the thrill of holding something in his hands from a time when whisky's future was still being shaped, and the delight in preserving things caught in a moment in time 'that were often never intended to have a life of more than a few weeks at most. They were truly *ephemeral*.'

Whisky, or so it seems, has something to offer to everyone. You can visit the places where it's made, the stunning locations of distilleries around the world. There are tourist attractions in Scotland and Kentucky to educate and entertain consumers. Drinkers can enjoy a range of tastes and textures without compare. You can join clubs and visit shows, digitally or in person. You can read books about it. Experts can collect facts, passionate enthusiasts can collect bottles, memorabilia or ephemera. If you're foolish enough you could blow your life's savings on one or other of the many highly speculative whisky investment schemes. As people who work in the industry will tell you, it can be, in the very best sense, life consuming. And the people who work in the industry are, let me tell you, very special.

WHISKY IN POPULAR CULTURE

'I'm only a common old working chap,
as anyone here can see, but when I get
a couple of drinks on a Saturday Glasgow
belongs to me.'

— Will Fyffe, 'I Belong to Glasgow'

Celebrated in song, prose and poetry; a staple of music-hall comedians, cartoonists and saucy seaside postcards; a constant in film from the earliest movies to *High Noon* and *Lost in Translation*, whisky has seamlessly cemented its place in popular culture around the world over the past three hundred years. In return, popular culture, like a distorting mirror, has played back ideas and images of whisky, whisky drinkers and whisky drinking that have become deeply etched in the cultural memory, passed on from generation to generation. Some of this process was begun by whisky makers themselves, particularly as widespread and sophisticated advertising for their products began to appear around the world in the late nineteenth century. But whisky had been available for a long time before that, and dogmas about its uses and consumption, benefits and dangers (many of which were influenced by state religion), popular belief and even folklore, were long-established. The ancient English ballad 'John Barleycorn', which even Burns produced a Scots version of, told the story of the cultivation, harvest, malting and milling of barley, and the consumption and enjoyment of the resulting alcoholic beverage, and the effects that had on the drinkers. It didn't specify the nature of the drink, beer, or malt spirit, but Burns seems to have taken it as whisky. Despite this remarkable ballad, whose haunting narrative still charms singers and musicians, it has to be said that as far as song is concerned Scotch, and whisky in general, has fared far less well than it has benefitted from the written word. Whisky songs are normally about drinking, drunkenness and the perils that follow. Listen, if you will, to the

Scottish 'Nancy Whisky', the Irish 'Whiskey in the Jar', or the American 'Cigarettes, Whiskey and Wild, Wild Women' and you'll hear the same predictable story being retold. Few songs elevate themselves beyond this, Leonard Cohen's 'Closing Time', which captures something of the poetry of moment, or the spirit of drinking whisky, being a notable exception. So, in this chapter it is principally words on the page, and associated wordsmiths, that will concern us.

BACK TO THE FUTURE ...

In the second half of the nineteenth century, whisky distillers and blenders backfilled their way into the popular culture of the past through carefully chosen brand names and imagery on packaging, promotional pieces and in advertising. In order to give legitimacy, and what we would today call 'heritage', to both the whisky category and their particular brands, these producers and their advertising agencies crafted an imagined past in which their brands lived and breathed. Old Crow, Old Quaker, My Old Kentucky Home, Old Kentucky Tavern, Elijah Craig and Colonel E. H. Taylor are some bourbon brands; Grand Old Parr, Iona, King George IV, Royal Household, Beau Brummel, Claymore, Ivanhoe are some Scotch blends. It was all about

Dewar's famously set their brand amidst pyramids with faux hieroglyphic fonts promising 'the whisky of great age', an example of the increasing sophistication of whisky advertising in the late Victorian and Edwardian periods.

placing your brand in a particular time; a place, a moment or with a person from the past, and appropriating the provenance that went with it. Antiquity also had the benefit of endowing whiskies of uncertain vintage and origin great apparent age and maturity. And for blenders from Scotland's increasingly overcrowded and unhealthy cities, the use of striking imagery stolen from elsewhere helped promote the purity of their product, clothed in tartan, heather and Highland kitsch. For those with the budgets and brains, the increasingly sophisticated advertising of the late Victorian and Edwardian period was even more powerful. Dewar's set their brand amidst pyramids, sphinxes and pharaohs with faux hieroglyphic fonts promising 'the whisky of great age'. Black and White was seen with an assortment of characters from Dickens's novels before visiting the famous old coaching houses of England. Johnnie Walker conversed and joked with a diverse group of friends from fact and fiction – Shakespeare, Mr Pickwick, John Halifax, Falstaff, Tom Faggus, Ben Jonson – in a 'literary series' of advertisements. The message was always the same. These new brands were as familiar in the past as they were in the present. They were aged, yet ageless. Nothing delivered this message more clearly than Dewar's 'The Whisky of his forefathers' – the scene, a kilted gentleman at a table overlooked by paintings of generations his forbears, who step off the canvas to join him in a celebratory toast. Print, posters, postcards, playing cards; the image was used widely and became one of the first motion picture advertisements for any product. This artificial history of the Real Mountain Dew was created at a stroke, and ironically was transformed into a golden age of Scotch that so many of the early writers to take on the subject longed for. But this was not the golden age of today's whisky enthusiasts, rather the golden age of those searching for Scotland's lost national identity.

The message was always the same. These new brands were as familiar in the past as they were in the present. They were aged, yet ageless.

There's something about words and whisky. Think about all those words crammed in very small print around a flavour wheel – each a whisky word to provoke a memory of a place, a person or a thing. Each single whisky word the mother or father of many others. Words tumbling down like a small highland spring that ends up as a wide meandering river heading to the ocean. An ocean of words. Whisky fires the imagination in the same way that it warms the soul. The places it comes from – be they wild and heartachingly beautiful, or urban iron-barred fortresses. The people who make it – proud, patrician, resilient and remarkable. The pleasure it provokes in good company or in companions remembered. Like stepping through a looking glass, whisky is a doorway to another world: a world we have gained, and a world we have lost. Hardly surprising that Robert Burns, in whose writing whisky was never too far away, should express his poet's gratitude in 'Scotch Drink', published in 1785: 'O Whisky! soul o' plays and pranks! Accept a bardie's gratfu' thanks!' Victorian authors on both sides of the Atlantic loved Scotch whisky and the colour it brought to characters and events; they also admired the Highlander's legendary prowess when it came to consumption, which even in temperance times was considered a sign of noble virtue. It recalled the heroic drinkers described by early Hebridean traveller Martin Martin, the 'chief lords of the isles', sitting in a circle, sharing usqebaugh from a quaich, until the last man among them dropped. It was almost as if there was a native innocence in this drinking, free as it was from the squalor of industrial slums and servitude. Scottish novelist William Black, 'whose name' said his biographer in 1902, 'was bracketed with those of the greatest novelists of the day', was an enthusiast for Highland air and Highland whisky and peppered his pages with references to Scotch, Lagavulin in particular, so much so that one might wonder if, like some twenty-first century 'influencer', he wasn't in the pay of distillery owners Mackie & Co. to promote their product. His words, from the short story *The Strange Horse of Loch Suainabhal*,

Early Scotch advertisements wanted to convey the message that the whiskies were aged, yet ageless. Print, posters, postcards, playing cards; the images from some of these adverts, especially Dewer's, were used widely and one even became one of the first motion picture advertisements for any product.

published in 1875, have long been on the label of Lagavulin whisky: 'I hef been close by the Lagavulin Distillery, and I know that it is the clear watter of the spring that will mek the Lagavulin whisky just as fine as the new milk'. Like Black, American author Sylvanus Cobb Jr, 'a prolific writer of sensational tales quite without literary value', wrote freely about whisky, particularly Lagavulin, in stories set in Scotland, where his characters could drink 'what would have intoxicated half a dozen Lowlanders, and killed as many Frenchmen'.

THE FATHER OF WHISKY WRITING

Many people today consider Alfred Barnard, author of *The Whisky Distilleries of the United Kingdom*, first published in 1887 by Sir Joseph Causton & Sons, the father of whisky writing. Born in 1837 Barnard appears to have worked in the wine trade before joining the *Wine and Spirit Gazette*, otherwise known as *Harper's Weekly*, as a 'correspondent' in the early 1880s. It was during a visit to Scottish distilleries in 1885 that Barnard 'was struck with the fact that the Whisky world in general was entirely ignorant of many, if not the whole of, the establishments from which the various makes of Whisky emanate'. This insight led him to spend much of the next two years visiting every distillery in the Kingdom (161 in total) and writing these visits up in the series of sketches that make up the book. Barnard described these visits with a purple pen, often taking up more words to describe the journey and scenery (and the occasional breakfast and lunch) than he did to describe the distilleries. His accounts of the distilleries, often with meticulously drawn illustrations, were always detailed, although some are sufficiently perfunctory to suggest he might not have actually visited all of them in person. At his best, he regales his readers with every available fact and measurement, like a modern metronomic distillery guide. Apart from volumetric data, there is not much to be said about the quality or character of so many of the whiskies that he saw being made, and often tasted. We know there were 'ball men' at some distilleries charged with monitoring both the strength and quality of new make spirit, but what that quality was remains for the most part a mystery. Lagavulin was a notable exception; not only did Barnard describe the eight-year-old whisky he tasted as 'remarkably fine', but he also pointed out that 'there are only a few of the Scotch distillers that turn out spirit for use as single whiskies, and that made at Lagavulin can claim to be the most prominent'. Barnard's work was welcomed by reviewers, Aberdeen's *Press and Journal* noting that he had done 'right in telling us where this nectar is made, and who are its most famous and extensive makers', recommending the book 'to that large and steadily increasing class who love good whisky'.

Two years after the publication of his distilling opus, Barnard produced the first of what would eventually be four volumes of *The Noted Breweries of Great Britain and Ireland*. Many of the individual chapters were republished as separate booklets for publicity purposes by the featured brewers. Not all the reviews for this work were as kind as those for the first. Barnard continued his association with *Harper's*, writing occasional updates on his original distillery visits for the magazine, and went on to publish at least ten small publicity booklets and brochures commissioned by various companies, including the soon-to-be imprisoned Patterson's, (whose blending business failed so spectacularly in 1899), Johnnie Walker, Watson's of Dundee and Mackie & Co., owners of Lagavulin distillery and the White Horse blend. He became the first whisky hack (now a large and noble profession) and, desperate to scrape a living, also spread his wings to other less liquid subjects. One of the projects, commissioned by the retailers William Whitely, and largely comprising photographs of their various food-related operations, from orchard and pigsties to jam factories and potted meats, received a derisory review from the *Glasgow Herald*. Few of the 50,000 copies printed were sold at the retail price of five shillings. Another, written for Greenlees Brothers, included a tourist's guided to Scottish golf courses. His last known publication was a guidebook to the city of Warwick.

SCOTS WHAE HAE!

The years from the publication of Barnard's *Whisky Distilleries* to the start of the Second World War saw the publication of only a handful of books relating to whisky. Nettleton's *The Manufacture of Whisky and Plain Spirit*, one of the most detailed technical handbooks on the subject, was published in 1903, the same year that Sir Walter Gilbey of W & A Gilbey published his *Notes on Alcohol in Brandy, Whisky and Rum*. Former Excise officer Ian MacDonald's reminiscences, *Smuggling in the Highlands*, were published in 1914, and then Aeneas MacDonald's Whisky in 1930, and the novelist Neil M. Gunn's *Whisky and Scotland* in 1935. *Whisky*, of which we have already heard, was a polemic written by George Malcolm Thomson, an early and influential supporter of the idea of cultural nationalism, who in the 1920s railed against the growing anglicisation of Scotland, and even more so the insidious influence of Roman Catholic Irish immigrants, who, he claimed, were taking over the body and soul of the nation. His book on whisky should be read in the light of this extreme political position. Although he was also a champion of cultural and political nationalism Gunn's book, subtitled *A Practical and Spiritual Survey*, adopted an entirely different, almost metaphysical approach, to the place of whisky in Scottish culture and history. Only a third of the book is really about the making or drinking of Scotch, the majority is a passionately written exploration of where Scotch whisky sits in the national psyche, and of its importance to being Scottish. Whisky was a drink that dealt 'in the colourless logic of truth', permitting 'no other attitude of mind'. It was as much the *idea* of the drink as its consumption, that shaped its influence on Scottish character. 'Whisky', said Gunn, 'isolates the human spirit in its native integrity, into its ultimate loneliness, and yet warms that loneliness with creative fire'. But, like MacDonald, and the writers who were to follow in a similar vein, most notably Sir Robert Bruce Lockhart and even David Daiches, Gunn (a former excise officer who knew whisky well) was a slave to an imagined past, a romantic notion of a golden age of whisky and of Scottish culture and nobility, which somehow had been stolen by the rise of blended Scotch. If one could return, then so could the other. Probably no one made this correlation more than poet Christopher Grieve (who wrote as Hugh MacDiarmid) father of the 'Scottish Renaissance' of the twentieth century and author of 'A Drunk Man Looks at the Thistle'. MacDiarmid despised popular culture with a snobbery that belied his own modest upbringing and circumstances, and in particular loathed comedian Harry Lauder, who's 'Wee Deoch-an-Doris', among other songs, had made him world famous and very wealthy. MacDiarmid had nothing but contempt for the comic drunkenness of Lauder's songs, or the common inebriation of the working man, yet of course was complicit in, and even celebrated, the sneering intoxication (naturally from single malts rather than blends) of the self-styled literary and political elites.

Nonetheless Gunn, MacDonald, Bruce Lockhart (*Scotch: The Whisky of Scotland in Fact and Story*) and Daiches (*Scotch Whisky: Its Past and Present*) should be on any word-loving whisky drinker's bookshelf. They are among the great books on whisky and for all their faults, are as timeless classics as a bottle of Glenfiddich or Johnnie Walker Black Label. They all refight the battles of the past, of malt against grain, malt distillers against blenders, and almost to a man show little understanding or interest in the nature of what was already a multi-million-pound industry of huge importance to Scotland and the British Exchequer. And, of course, they established that tramway of tropes slavishly followed by some enthusiasts today, with their shared enthusiasm for a lost world

that never quite existed. But they are books written with *heart*, not least Bruce Lockhart's book, with its reminiscences of childhood days spent at Balmenach distillery on Speyside, and as such are worthy of admiration and time well spent in enjoying them. The publication of Daiches' book in 1969, just at that tipping point of both interest and availability of single malts in the UK and Europe, heralded a surge in whisky writing. If, as we have seen, those writing about the taste of whisky at the time were mostly women, those turning out the books were exclusively men. Among these was Ross Wilson, scholar and public relations man who had a spell with the Scotch Whisky Association, looms large with *Scotch Made Easy* (1959), *Scotch: The Formative Years* (1970) and *Scotch: Its History and Romance* (1973); Wilson also authored a company history of William Sanderson & Sons, *The House of Sanderson*, makers of the famous Vat 69 blend, often said to be the Pope's favourite whisky. *Scotch: The Formative Years* is a detailed and very well-informed history that was only supplanted with the publication of *The Making of Scotch Whisky* by Michael S. Moss and John R. Hume in 1981. With a detail of scholarly research not formerly seen in whisky publications, and now in its second edition, this became the standard reference for

The Vat 69 blend by William Sanderson was often said to be the Pope's favourite whisky.

∧

Whisky is not just about fact and there is an honourable tradition of whisky fiction that the enthusiast can explore and enjoy.

those interested in whisky's past. An equally scholarly work that needs to be read in order to understand the current shape and structure of the industry is Ron Weir's *The History of the Distiller's Company 1877–1939*; this is a proper piece of economic and business history, so just be warned that although the author, an academic at the University of York, was one of the most jovial you could ever wish to meet, his book is slightly short on jokes. One final title to mention here is Allen Andrews's entertaining *The Whisky Barons* (1977) a biographical history of Scotch seen through the lives of those ennobled entrepreneurs who shaped Scotch during the late Victorian and Edwardian eras.

THE WHISKY MURDERS ...

Whisky is not just about fact and there is an honourable tradition of whisky fiction that the enthusiast can explore and enjoy. Foremost among whisky novels must be *Whisky Galore* (1947) written by Compton Mackenzie, a First World War spy for the British army in Greece, an ardent Scottish Nationalist, and prolific author. The novel tells the tale of the wreck of a cargo vessel, holds brimming with whisky bound for the United States, off the islands of Great and Little Todday (Barra and Eriskay in the Outer Hebrides). Starved of whisky due to post-war restrictions the island's residents row out to the wreck, frustrated only by the turn of the Sabbath, and empty the holds of their cargoes of blended Scotch. They combine to outwit the head of the local Home Guard and convey much of the contraband to various hiding places around the island. Love is in the air, and the subsequent celebrations are, to say the least, well-lubricated. The story was based on the foundering of a real ship, the *SS Politician*, off Eriskay, in 1941. *SS Politician* was carrying whisky to the USA, but also currency bound for the Caribbean; as the locals helped themselves to whisky some also took banknotes that soon found their way into circulation in mainland Scotland and England, a part of the story not told by Mackenzie. Nor was the fact that a number of imprisonments followed the liberation of the whisky and cash. Mackenzie's book was adapted into a film directed by Alexander Mackendrick in 1949. Interest still surrounds the story and it's not unusual for bottles claiming to come from *SS Politician* to turn up at whisky auctions although one can be sure that the residents of Eriskay and the surrounding islands ensured that not a drop of salvaged whisky went undrunk. As a postscript in the 1950s Mackenzie appeared in a series of press adverts for Grant's Stand Fast, alongside Scottish literary stalwarts such as Sir Robert Bruce Lockhart and Eric Linklater.

Scotch whisky was a recurring fixture in much now forgotten crime fiction. The plots always had a strong romantic theme, where love laid the path for the redemption of the lead male character, often some sort of outsider. They also reflected a growing anxiety about change in the industry, the growth of corporate ownership, the incursion of foreign capital into the business, the vulnerability of small remote communities, and the impact of new technologies. Maurice Walsh's *The Key Above the Door* (1926) might not quite count as a whisky novel, but a considerable part of this love story is played out in and around Talisker Distillery on Skye. Walsh had followed the literary tradition established by Burns and served as an excise officer in Speyside where he became a friend of Neil Gunn; his most famous novel was *The Quiet Man*. In *A Sop O' Moonshine* (1931) John MacCallum (probably a pseudonym) tells the story of a laird's attempt to close Garryvore Distillery against the background of Prohibition in the United States, with a subplot of a love story involving the distillery owner's impossibly beautiful daughter. This more or less is the basis of all the novels that followed. In *The Great River* by James Wood (1955) a returned serviceman with a past to hide gets involved in trying to stop a conspiracy to bring Speyside distilling to its knees by contaminating malted barley with Khapra beetles, in the course of which he falls in love with the distillery manager's impossibly beautiful daughter. In 1979 disgraced senior Scottish Civil Servant George Pottinger published *Whisky Sour*, which he may well have started writing when he was in prison serving a sentence for his part in a massive corruption scandal, having taken bribes (including a purpose-built house next door to what is now Donald Trump's golf course at Muirfield) from architect John Poulson. With all that time on his hands Pottinger played a little with the otherwise reliable formula, a distillery on Skye, Old Portree whisky, the Laird's family divided, a reluctant hero, rare minerals, a millionaire American speculator, the shadow of incest, and Fiona, not a distillery manager's daughter, but nonetheless impossibly beautiful. Two thrillers by Richard Grayson, pseudonym for Richard Grindal who had worked for the Scotch Whisky Association for many years, and published many crime novels, along with a couple of whisky books under his own name, followed the same pattern. *Death Stalk* (1982) and *The Whisky Murders* (1984) involve an island distillery subject to a ruthless American takeover, a revolutionary new patented method of rapidly maturing whisky (a storyline based on real events that had taken place in the 1950s), several murders, a couple of reluctantly heroic men, and two impossibly beautiful distillery daughters. Like the whisky that flowed from the stills, the distillery owner's daughters were always impossibly beautiful. Stepping outside of this formula was John Quigley who published

Like the whisky that flowed from the stills, the distillery owner's daughters were always impossibly beautiful.

his *King's Royal* in 1975, the story of a Glasgow whisky-blending empire torn asunder by family rivalries and financial speculation. This, and the follow up *Queen's Royal* (1977), were made into a successful BBC costume drama in the early 1980s. In an example of truth being stranger than fiction, the well-known Glasgow blending company William Teacher's launched a King's Royal brand of Scotch whisky after the first novel had been published in the 1970s, and when it came to making the TV show in the 1980s the Scotch Whisky Association tried (but failed) to prevent the BBC from using the original name, as it had become a trademark.

THEY'RE GONNA PUT ME IN THE MOVIES ...

Of course, it's probably true that nothing has done more to propagate and perpetuate myths and stereotypes about whisky in popular culture than film and TV. They have certainly done more than any other media, including brand advertising, to publicise an almost exclusively masculine image of whisky that we see played back to us on big and small screens alike. It's not an image that stands up to the reality of today's drinkers, where perhaps a third or more of all whisky drinkers are women, and quite possibly never has, but it's one that the film industry in particular persists with. Whisky drinkers are fighters. Bar-room brawlers. Bullying wife beaters. The last man standing. Warriors. Enemies, united in the moment before battle by booze. Men seeking solace in a glass from the memory of fallen comrades. They are the long-standing cliché of the drunken detective – the solo sleuth whose only companion is the casually consumed cocktail or the carefully chosen single malt Scotch. Always free from female companionship, the bottle their only friend. It's about guns, gangsters and G-men; the road to perdition. Scotch is dangerous.

When the whisky is served you know something bad is going to happen. Whisky is the ultimate man's anaesthetic: 'pour me a shot and pour the rest over my wound before you operate on me with that rusty penknife'. Think of women and whisky in the movies and television and once you've got past Sugar Kane's hip flask in *Some Like it Hot*, or Joan Holloway's whiskey and coke (most likely Canadian Club) in *Mad Men* you may end up in *Skyfall* with a frightened and bruised woman with a glass of ludicrously expensive fifty-year-old malt whisky on her head being murdered by a psychopath, in a warped replay of William Tell shooting an apple off his child's head. Is it surprising that women sometimes don't feel welcomed in the world of whisky? Strong voices are now making sure that that will no longer be the case. Following on from the massive success of *Mad Men*, Joan Holloway actor Christina Hendricks went on to appear in a very successful advertising campaign for Johnnie Walker Black Label. She didn't get shot.

Following on from the massive success of *Mad Men* Joan Holloway actor Christina Hendricks went on to appear in a very successful advertising campaign for Johnnie Walker Black Label.

⌄

One film that cannot escape mention is Ken Loach's *The Angels' Share*, released in 2012. It tells the story of an unlikely group of four inner-city ne'er-do-wells from Glasgow who are mentored into whisky by a probation officer, who discovers that one of them possesses a rare talent for nosing and describing whiskies. Against a background of gang violence and domestic upheavals the four get involved in a chase to acquire the only surviving known cask of whisky from the Malt Mill distillery, which they learn, is about to be auctioned. This is fiction meeting fact, a common enough occurrence, as we shall see. Malt Mill was established within the grounds of Lagavulin Distillery on Islay by Peter Mackie in 1908 as a result of a long-term dispute with the owners of neighbouring Laphroaig distillery. Mackie had just lost the agency to distribute and sell Laphroaig whisky, and his intention was to make an identical spirit at the new distillery. The tiny Malt Mill, which only had an annual output of 560 butts, closed in 1962, so were a cask to survive it would be at least fifty years old. It is the great, legendary, unknown whisky. There is some considerable doubt as to whether the miniature of Malt Mill tasted by Serge Valentin and his chums a few years ago was genuine. Apart from this no one has ever tasted it, or at least none of today's wealthy collectors, investors and whisky experts. At a time when single bottles of rare whisky sell for over a million pounds it's hard to imagine what a cask of Malt Mill might realise were one ever to be found and put on sale. In collector's language, it would be a real unicorn. Dressing themselves in ill-fitting kilts, the protagonists set off for the distillery where the auction will be held under the unlikely guise of the Carntyne Malt Whisky Club. Predictable semi-comic shenanigans follow that form a path to redemption for the main character and his friends. Critical to the film is the role of world-leading whisky expert Rory McAllister, played by world-leading whisky expert Charlie MacLean, on whom scriptwriter Paul Laverty based the character. MacLean's performance was described by one critic as 'extraordinary'.

LOST IN TRANSLATION

Lost in Translation, starring Bill Murray as a famous actor sent to Tokyo to make an advertising film for Suntory whisky, had a great impact on the reputation of Japanese whisky and gave a huge boost to Suntory sales.

Look hard and you will find some great whisky films or scenes in films. Dewar's have to be recognised here for that first with the *Whisky of his Forefathers* advert, that allegedly brought New York to a standstill when it was projected onto a screen on top of a building facing Herald Square in 1892. *Whisky Galore!* is a homage to the water of life but its most compelling scene is probably on the deck of the *SS Cabinet Minister*, as the villagers stare wide-eyed into the hold at case after case of whisky, piled high like a dragon's treasure. *Lost in Translation*, starring Bill Murray as a famous actor sent to Tokyo to make an advertising film for Suntory whisky, will strike a special chord with anyone in the business who's ever had to have their photograph taken, or be filmed, holding a glass of whisky, not just in Japan, but anywhere in the world. Aside from that, it's also very funny. Incidentally, the film gave a huge boost to the reputation of Japanese whisky, and Suntory sales. *Get Shorty*, released in 1995, saw John Travolta's character, loan shark Chilli Palmer, navigate key scenes with Gene Hackman, playing a debt-ridden movie director, with the help of a bottle of Dewar's. Johnnie Walker Black Label adopted a modernistic bottle in *Blade Runner* when it was drunk by android-hunting detective Rick Deckard. Fiction again became reality when the brand produced a limited edition of the bottle to coincide with the release of *Blade Runner 2049*, now much sought after on the secondary market. Sister brand Johnnie Walker Red Label has been a constant companion to films, from the village pub in *Whisky Galore!* to the captain's quarters on the German battleship *Graf Spee* in *The Battle of the River Plate*, and from Harry Palmer's (played by actor Michael Caine) kitchen in *The Ipcress File* to Superman's local in *Superman III*, where devoid of his powers, Christopher Reeve's 'Man of Steel' succumbs to several shots of Scotch. When he wasn't drinking gin and tonics or vodka martinis James Bond had quite a preference for bourbon, and Roger Moore's 007 certainly got through a lot of Old Grand Dad in *Live and Let Die*. A final word on the subject: if you've ever been foolish enough to think of bourbon for breakfast

Johnnie Walker Black Label was android-hunting detective Rick Deckard's drink of choice in the movie *Blade Runner* and the brand later produced a limited edition of the bottle to coincide with the release of *Blade Runner 2049*, now much sought after on the secondary market.

then Jack Nicholson's reaction to his first pull of the day from a bottle of Jim Beam in *Easy Rider* is probably enough to change your mind forever.

'HAVE YOU SEEN MY WHISKY BOOK COLLECTION?'

There has, needless to say, been an exponential increase in the number of books published about whisky, Scotch and others, since 1980. Indeed one might wonder what, with the exception of this small volume of course, is left to be said on the subject. To make things a little more manageable let's start with the almanacs, companions, bibles, compendiums and handbooks. These list, describe and sometimes give points to bottlings, and mostly but not exclusively, single malts. In an Internet and mobile-device-fuelled world these publications may seem increasingly archaic, but the contribution they have collectively made to raising the awareness of different brands of whiskies and also educating consumers in the language of taste cannot be overstated. Wallace Milroy's role in starting this fashion with the *Malt Whisky Almanac* has already been acknowledged, as has Michael Jackson's with his *Malt Whisky Companion*. Since his death in 2007, Jackson's book has been updated regularly by journalist Dominic Roskrow and writer Gavin D. Smith. Of equal importance in terms of outreach to consumers has been Jim Murray's *Whisky Bible*, the annual editions of which (normally preceded by some clever headline-grabbing story that reaches the national press) are eagerly anticipated by some. In previous years, Murray's quite arbitrarily awarded 'Whisky of the Year' has been enough to empty shelves and fire-up secondary market speculation. It remains to be seen whether or not a controversy in 2020 about his long-standing use of sexual metaphors to describe whiskies will have dented his reputation. A slightly different take on the

Dominic Roskrow's *1001 Whiskies You Must Try Before You Die* offers the author's selection of some of the best whiskies to have been released, rather like an off-the-shelf bucket list for the enthusiast with deep pockets.

genre is the list book, like Ian Buxton's *101 Whiskies to Try Before You Die*, at the time of writing in its fourth edition, and Dominic Roskrow's characteristically ambitious *1001 Whiskies You Must Try Before You Die*, both offering the author's selection of some of the best whiskies to have been released, rather like an off-the-shelf bucket list for the enthusiast with deep pockets. It's in books like this that the reputations of whiskies can be made or broken, though it has to be said that most authors, not wishing to upset the whisky companies for whom they might often profitably consult, are very gentle in their comments. Murray is an exception, often sharing more strongly worded comments, for example about the presence of sulphur in certain malt whiskies. On the subject of tasting notes and points it is probably useful to know that many magazines, when rating new whiskies on a ten-point scale, refuse to allow their writers to score anything below a seven. The industry consensus is that, as the song had it, everything is beautiful in its own way.

On top of these mostly pocketbook-sized volumes (not Roskrow's, obviously) there are what we might call guides, like Dave Broom's *Handbook of Whisky* or *Whisky: The Manual*, or Charlie MacLean's beautifully illustrated *Malt Whisky* and *Spirit of Place* which offer the curious reader a little bit of everything. Rather like this book, they cover the history of whisky, detail the technical side of its production, offer advice on tasting, sensory analysis and drinking, and include a few lists too. And for those who can't easily get to Scotland or a distillery they bring to life through photography or drawings the hugely impactful visual aspect of whisky making, both in terms of the places, people and plant. Both Broom and MacLean share the passion for Scotch and Scotland so strongly displayed by their forebears, but these new books have far more detail around production, and in particular how that impacts on taste and what a reader might actually go and buy to drink. That represents one of the most significant shifts in writing over recent years, and in turn indicates not just the level of thirst that exists for this sort of information, but also the willingness of the industry in general to open its doors to writers and journalists. Some call it transparency. Even thirty years ago Scotch producers were likely to put up the shutters with a disdainful 'why does anyone want to know that?' when asked difficult questions. Now they fall over themselves to provide the sort of data that finds its way into annual publications such as Ingvar Ronde's invaluable *Malt Whisky Yearbook*, as well as the sort of book that Broom or MacLean might write. There are also some exceptionally useful technical publications for the real geek to paw over, such as Inge Russell's *Whisky: Technology, Production and Marketing*, and Ian Buxton and Paul S. Hughes' *The Science and Commerce of Whisky*.

There are also a number of relatively recently published brand and distillery histories, but they need to be treated with a degree of caution. Some are written by well-meaning enthusiasts with little scholarly skill, others read like old-fashioned company histories, and just occasionally the hand of the marketing department can be seen gently massaging the past to align it with current brand stories. At least, one might argue, the amateurs are beyond the reach of the distiller's pocket. The majority of writers and journalists are dependent on whisky makers not just for information and access to distilleries, but also for whisky samples and very often lucrative consultancy work. The intimacy that they seek with producers, and that producers seek with them, can lead to uncomfortable questions about the degree of independence that exists in their writing. It's certainly true for example, that those whisky magazines that have appeared over the past thirty years, dependent as they are on advertising, rarely rock the boat when it

The industry consensus is that, as the song had it, everything is beautiful in its own way.

comes to serious industry issues. Few, if any, have an appetite for taking on issues that are of genuine importance for consumers.

If some of this makes you worry about the future of whisky writing, then consider the final genre of books to be discussed. Broadly speaking let's call it the whisky travelogue although, as will become apparent, at its best it's far more than that. Of course, it did all start with Alfred Barnard whose sometimes detailed descriptions of distilleries were interspersed with personal observations on local history and scenery, recollections of chit-chat with local cabmen and coachmen, and lugubrious particulars about his mode of travel. Barnard's journey was a personal pilgrimage, and he made it so even in the pages of a book intended for the trade. In recent years the personal whisky journey has produced some of the more interesting and entertaining books, which offer joyous release from facts, figures and a few more facts and figures. The trend may have started as far back as 1985 with Neil Wilson's *Scotch & Water*, which was followed up by *The Island Whisky Trail* in 2003, both compelling Hebridean odysseys. Broadcaster Tom Morton took to a motorbike in his *Spirit of Adventure: A Journey Beyond the Whisky Trails*, first published in 1992, author Iain Banks chose a feisty 1965 Jaguar Mark II 3.5 for his search for the perfect whisky in *Raw Spirit*, published in 2003. Andrew Jefford didn't get further than Islay for his *Peat Smoke and Spirit*, published the following year, while Hans Offringa travelled *The Road to Craigellachie* in 2005, and again in 2011. More recently writer and broadcaster Rachel McCormack went *Chasing the Dram*, which involved a train journey to Kilmarnock, and Ian Buxton published his *Whiskies Galore: A Tour of Scotland's Island Distilleries*, an expedition largely facilitated by ferry operators Caledonian MacBrayne. These books are all very different but they bring to the reader personality, passion (even from Ian Buxton, who claims to despise the word), intimate insights and not a small amount of humour, something that is sadly lacking in some of the 'dry as dust' books. The personal whisky memoir, well authored, offers a rich furrow for writers to explore.

THE BEST WHISKY WRITER?

When we asked people associated with the whisky business around the world who their favourite writers were there was a clear consensus that Dave Broom and Charlie MacLean take the crown. If you're thinking of starting a whisky library, or even worse a whisky book collection, you could do worse than start with these two. Charlie tends to focus more on the past, Dave on understanding how the past has shaped the present. Charlie is a Scotch man, Dave has spread his wings and written about whiskies across the world, as well as gin and rum. They are both impeccable tasters and in addition to consultancy work for producers they contribute tasting notes to magazines and websites (Dave has his own). The late Michael Jackson, whose *Whisky Companion* did so much to fuel the growth of interest in single malt Scotch got a more than honourable mention, and deservedly so. Like Broom and MacLean do, Jackson wrote beautifully – not just words on the page but something more. When Kurt Maitland spoke of Dave Broom he simply said 'I love the poetry of his writing'; Billy Abbott added 'he doesn't really ever write about whisky. It's always about the things around the whisky that make it important, different and special.' Also in the mix were Ian Buxton, Dominic Roskrow, Gavin Smith, Liza Weisstuch, Whiskyfun's Serge Valentin and Angus MacRaild. When it came to 'what is your favourite book?' the answers were more diverse. Dave Broom, Rachel McCormack and Serge Valentin opted for David Daiches's *Scotch Whisky*; 'he had the old-fashioned cultured man tone and did it beautifully,' said Rachel. Broom's view was 'beautifully written (as you would expect from a Professor of English), concise and with an eye on the bigger picture. Also, a great snapshot of how people viewed whisky in the late 1960s.' Annabel Meikle, Director of the Keepers of the Quaich, chose Neil Gunn's *Whisky and Scotland* while Richard Woodard picked 'Robert Bruce Lockhart for writing *Scotch*, which I adore for all its partiality'. Charlie MacLean was not the only person to opt for Aeneas MacDonald. Bernhard Schaffer chose Wallace Milroy's *Malt Whisky Almanac*, explaining 'of course it's outdated, but one has to see the pioneering work of that book and Wallace was one of the most gentle men I had the pleasure to meet'. Schaffer also put in a good word for *The Schweppes Guide to Scotch*, written by Philip Morrice; auction director Isabel Graham-Yooll said 'the whisky books I've enjoyed most are the niche passion projects written by whisky enthusiasts or extremists. However it's probably *The Schweppes Guide* that I've referred back to most often.' Japanese whisky journalist, translator, collector and bottler Hideo Yamaoka chose Michael Jackson's *Whisky Companion* and his 2005 publication *Whisky*, both of which he translated into Japanese. Some books divided opinion: Billy Abbott loved Iain Banks's *Raw Spirit*, commenting 'it's not a book about whisky. It's about driving cars on the great wee roads of Scotland, hanging out with your mates and drinking red wine …'. Richard Woodard wrote '*De mortuis nil nisi bonum*, but I read *Raw Spirit* by Iain Banks a year or two ago, and was hugely disappointed by it. I really wanted to like it…'. The Whisky Exchange's Sukhinder Singh admired Andrew Jefford's exquisitely written love poem to Islay, *Peat Smoke and Spirit*. Editor, writer and bass player Rob Allanson chose 'Hans Offringa's series on music and whisky – just lovely reads'.

The personal whisky memoir, well authored, offers a rich furrow for writers to explore.

WHISKY PEOPLE

09

'The mashman has been thirty years brewing at Lagavulin, and succeeded his father who, for over forty years before him, held the same post until he handed down the secrets to his son.'

— Alfred Barnard, *How to Blend Scotch Whisky*, c.1898

There is something special about whisky that seems to attract special people. Talk to anyone in the business, anywhere in the world, and they'll tell you it's a people industry. Some are born to it, either into long-standing family businesses which they join and manage, or simply born into a family tradition in a town or village where the local distillery happens to be the major employer. George Grant, currently sales director of Glenfarclas, represents the sixth generation to work at the family business. Iain MacArthur, quite possibly the most famous distillery worker in the world, chose to work first at Islay's Port Ellen distillery and then Lagavulin, because he was born just down the road, and, like George Grant, he was following in the footsteps of previous generations. Others are business professionals, accountants, marketeers, salesmen and scientists brought into the whisky world for their specialisms, but soon bitten by the whisky bug, finding they just can't let go. Occasionally someone, like the author, arrives just by happy accident and never leaves – a bit like an unwanted guest at Christmas. People make whisky, people shape its destiny, people sell it to the world, and people drink and enjoy it. Marketeers used to talk about the 'three Ps' of Scotch: real products, from real places, made by real people. The people who make Scotch, or Bourbon, or Canadian, Japanese and Irish whiskey have a huge passion for what they do, and they are immensely proud of the whiskies they produce. So are the people who sell it. Be assured that this passion exists no more or less at large companies than it is does small. Despite what they may suggest the johnny-come-lately new-age distiller has no monopoly on passion. It's a passion that comes from the heart, not from the head. Whisky is a spirit of the soul, whether by birth or bite, an all-encompassing spirit that can drive remarkable people to think and do remarkable things. And very often these remarkable people have remarkable personalities. 'Larger than life' is the accepted cliché. This chapter looks at a somewhat randomly selected handful of the men and women from the past and the present who have helped to make whisky's reputation around the world: distillers, distillery workers, blenders, marketeers, taste makers, retailers, bar owners. Some of them have very public faces and are either well known in history or well known in today's world of whisky. Others from the past have been forgotten, or from more recent years were relatively unknown to the public yet had huge reputations and influence within the industry. And they are, almost entirely, those people *in* the industry rather than those who choose to inhabit its periphery. Needless to say there is no shortage of rising stars among the new generation of whisky makers, like Annabel Thomas at the very modern Nc'nean, 'whisky bonder' Louise McGuane at J J Corry, or David Vitale at Starward. Time will tell if they last the course. For a balanced view, we also asked our group of expert commentators to choose their favourite and most influential figures from yesterday and today.

Be assured that this passion exists no more or less at large companies than it is does small. Despite what they may suggest the johnny-come-lately new-age distiller has no monopoly on passion. It's a passion that comes from the heart, not from the head.

SHADOWS FROM THE PAST

If the popular narrative around whisky today is driven by single malt Scotches, new start-up distilleries all around the world and the need for greater diversity in 'the industry', then the narrative of the past is dominated principally by the great men of blended whisky. As we have seen they are often, somewhat unhelpfully, described as the 'whisky barons', which suggests a far more collective and coherent group of entrepreneurs than actually existed. But fate has decreed that the Ushers, Walkers, Mackies, Dewars and Buchanans, who straddled the Victorian and Edwardian eras will forever be grouped together despite their considerable differences. Globally their counterparts might be George T Stagg or Isaac Wolfe Bernheim from Kentucky, Hiram Walker from Canada, the Jamesons and Roes from Dublin, and the Japanese Masataka Taketsuru and Shinjiro Torii. Due to the dramatic changes in the structure of the Scotch industry in the first decades of the twentieth century, many brands and even more people are largely forgotten, but a few should be brought back into memory for the lasting contributions they made. The Greenlees Brothers, distillers from Campbeltown, moved to London in the early 1870s to grow their Scotch blending business. Their brand Lorne Whisky vied with Walker's Old Highland for leadership in the crucial London market in the 1880s and 1890s. Of the two brothers, James and Samuel, it was James who appeared as an industry spokesperson at both the Select Committee on British and Foreign Spirits in 1891 and the Royal Commission on Whisky in 1908; of all the whisky witnesses he was the most eloquent. Highly influential in trade and political circles, he also represented the industry in discussions on duties and taxation. In March 1900 he hosted a visit to Greenlees Brothers' bond by the Chinese Ambassador to the Court of St James, who was moved to say 'that by taking whisky they [the Chinese people] would be enabled to replace

The Greenlees Brothers, distillers from Campbeltown, moved to London in the early 1870s to grow their Scotch blending business. Their brand Lorne Whisky vied with Walker's Old Highland for leadership in the crucial London market in the 1880s and 1890s.

Peter Dawson managed to get whisky taken on various scientific expeditions, including Captain Scott's doomed trek to the South Pole in 1910; undeterred by its failure, Dawson added the line 'a reputation which extends from John O'Groats to the South Pole' to his advertising.

other vices such as opium smoking. He thought that spirit always made people jolly while opium made them sleepy'. Their distillery at Hazelburn was a frequent port of call for guests on the Royal Yacht during West Highland cruises. Samuel Greenlees, known as 'the whisky millionaire' was a great enthusiast for showbusiness, and after he retired became one of the principal financiers of what is now known as Shepperton Studios. The Greenlees Brothers brand Grand Old Parr is still part of the Diageo portfolio, rarely seen in the UK, but selling over a million cases a year in Latin America.

Peter Dawson was the third generation of his family to run his distilling and blending business, he had owned Auchnagie distillery near Pitlochry, and in the boom years of the 1890s was one of the principal promoters of the construction of Convalmore and Towiemore distilleries. At the heart of his business was blending, with brands such as Old Curio and Dawson's Special which were sold throughout the Empire, and beyond. Described as a 'metatherian blender of exquisite potations,' Dawson never failed to find opportunities to promote his brands, achieving great publicity when he made up a massive blend of 12,370 gallons of Scotch in Glasgow, 'which represented the matured products of twenty-five first class stills'. He managed to get whisky taken on various scientific expeditions, including Captain Scott's doomed trek to the South Pole in 1910; undeterred by its failure, he added the line 'a reputation which extends from John

The narrative of the past is dominated principally by the great men of blended whisky

O'Groats to the South Pole' to his advertising. In 1919
he sponsored a crew to take part in the 'great air race' from
England to Australia, purchasing a war-surplus single-engine
biplane for the two-man crew to fly, carrying with them a
bottle of his whisky to be presented to the Premier of New
South Wales. They completed the trip, not without many
hazards, in 206 days. Dawson had travelled the world widely
on whisky business and was persuaded that too much investment
in advertising inevitably led to a deterioration in the quality of
the whisky being sold. He felt strongly that the aim of increasing
trade was to put the quality inside rather than outside the bottle.
Like Greenlees Brothers, Dawson had built up substantial stocks
of maturing whisky and when the value of these liquid assets
boomed after the First World War they both took advantage
of the potential profits and sold up to the DCL whose blending
companies were hungry for Scotch. In the process they more
or less disappeared from the stage of whisky history.

In 1919 Peter
Dawson sponsored
a crew to take part
in the 'great air
race' from England
to Australia,
purchasing a
war-surplus single-
engine biplane for
the two-man crew
to fly, carrying with
them a bottle of
his whisky to be
presented to the
Premier of New
South Wales. They
completed the trip
in 206 days.

PETER
DAWSON
SPECIAL

PD

THE LOYAL DISTILLERS

Long John McDonald of Ben Nevis's eponymous brand was one of the most popular single malts of the mid-1800's. He received permission from the Queen to gift the Prince of Wales a cask of whisky that would be kept at Buckingham Palace until he came of age.

For all the celebrity enjoyed by these successful blenders, and the acclaim that distilleries such as Glenlivet received, the men who made the whisky were virtually anonymous outside the localities where they held sway. Two exceptions in the nineteenth century were John Begg of Lochnagar and Long John McDonald of Ben Nevis, whose eponymous brands, along with Peter Mackie's Lagavulin, were probably the most popular single malts of the day. Their fame sprang from the growing fashion for travel in the Highlands, which accelerated rapidly after Queen Victoria acquired the Balmoral estate and built a new residence there in 1852. McDonald, a giant of a man, was already famous: both for his highly publicised adventures on Ben Nevis, after which his distillery was named, and other local mountains; and for the patronage bestowed on his whisky by both the royal family, very much the focus of the public's attention, and the aristocracy. He had been involved in a dramatic night-time rescue of the Duchess of Buccleuch from the mountain in 1838, which had brought his name to national attention, and in 1847 he acted as guide for Prince Waldemar of Prussia when he climbed Ben Nevis during a visit to Scotland which had also included Iona and Staffa. In the same year, when the child was only six, he received permission from the Queen to gift the Prince of Wales a cask of whisky that would be kept at Buckingham Palace until he came of age. In January 1850 he began advertising his celebrated whisky for sale in London.

At Lochnagar distillery, John Begg was the Queen's neighbour at Balmoral and hosted innumerable visits from the sovereign herself, and also her many visitors (and relatives) from Europe's royal families. After Queen Victoria's first visit with Prince Albert and her children in September 1848 the *Sun* recorded that 'the Prince tasted the result of the operation he had witnessed and the Queen condescendingly put it to her lips', pronouncing 'the

quality to be very fine'. Like British holidaymakers at a Spanish bodega, they ordered a few cases to take home, and also awarded Begg a Royal Warrant. By November, Royal Lochnagar whisky was being advertised in the *Morning Post* and the *Lady's Own Magazine,* who declared it to be 'perfectly pure, so fine in flavour and such exquisite bouquet'. Early the following year, Begg reported his whisky sales had increased immensely since the Queen's visit, warning consumers to beware of counterfeits. His celebrity assured, as newspapers and magazines always reported, he was graced with visits from the Queen at his distillery and his home (for tea and cake) when she was at Balmoral, and regularly dined and drank with princes and politicians at the castle, for whom his whisky was no doubt an ameliorative from the dreaded dullness of the Scottish visits.

MACHIAVELLIANS AND MOBSTERS

As the Edwardians turned into Georgians and the giants of the industry, those 'whisky barons' of such fame, slowly faded from view the lean inter-war years seemed to witness a decline in the number of prominent personalities in the whisky business. The Scotch industry was being shaped and led by one man, W H Ross of the Distillers Company, who with a high-starched collar and dour demeanour did not provide a compelling face of the industry. Sir Alexander Walker, less publicity shy than Ross, politically connected, a philanthropist and patron of the arts, was the only survivor of the great men of the large brand-owning companies who made it through to the war. Their successors were less flamboyant, more risk averse and a little monotone. The profits and dramas of the Prohibition period were shrouded with an understandable discreteness, although Eddie Tatham's exploits and adventures in the United States were responsible for laying the foundations of J&B's great success there, in the wake of the launch of Cutty Sark by their rivals Berry Brothers, from the other side of St James's. In Canada, Samuel Bronfman emerged from Prohibition to shape a world-leading drinks business, specialising in Canadian, American and Scotch whiskies, which would relocate its head offices to the Seagram Building in New York in the 1950s. His deadliest rival was Lewis 'Lew' Rosenstiel, who along with Joseph Reinfeld had been part of the distribution network employed by Bronfman to get whisky and gin into the United States in the 1920s and 1930s. Rosenstiel had acquired a number of distilleries during Prohibition, and at repeal founded the Schenley Company, who became US distributors of Dewar's Scotch. Among his business associates were the 'colourful' Frank Costello, Sam Giacana and Meyer Lansky. Rosenstiel had acquired substantial parcels of Jack Daniel's whiskey during the Prohibition years but his attempts to sell them after 1933 were frustrated by the trademark owner Len Motlow. Motlow's trademark was for the 'Old No 7' brand, so Rosenstiel named his 'Old No 8'. Later, having been beaten to the purchase of Jack Daniel's in 1958 by Brown Forman, he rebuilt the George Dickel distillery in Tennessee, and not to be outdone by Jack named that whiskey 'No 8' too. Both Bronfman and Rosenstiel built up huge corporations and massive fortunes, they were both domineering and ruthless personalities, but it was very probably Bronfman's obsession with quality as compared to Rosenstiel's with sales that marked the difference between the two when it came to the success and longevity of their brands. At the end of the day, it was Bronfman who came out on top.

KEEP IT IN THE FAMILY

Despite the dominance of the DCL in the UK and the growing Scotch whisky interests of Bronfman and Rosenstiel, and Canada's Hiram Walker, small privately owned businesses still played a

significant role in whisky distilling, and would be poised to take advantage of the rapidly changing business environment in the 1970s and 1980s. In 1951 Charlie Gordon qualified as an accountant from the University of Glasgow and joined the family business, William Grant, distillers of Glenfiddich and Balvenie, and owners of the successful blend Stand Fast. In 1953 he became a director and, along with his brother Sandy, transformed the business, taking full advantage of the opening up of the whisky trade from post-war restrictions. He was heavily involved in the marketing drive behind Glenfiddich in the early 1960s, and the introduction of the brand into numerous export markets and the new world of duty-free retail; taking it to New York in 1969 in combative style: 'if I can annoy 90 per cent of the market and have 10 per cent that's alright with me'. He was also determined to maintain the independence of his business in the face of the giant Distillers Company by freeing them from the grip the DCL had on the supply of grain whisky. This led to the construction of Girvan distillery in 1963, where a malt whisky distillery, Ladyburn, was added in 1966; as demand outstripped supply for 12-year-old Glenfiddich he could see that building up whisky stocks was the key to long-term success. It was not without reason that he earned the sobriquet 'Mr Scotch Whisky'. On Islay, Elizabeth 'Bessie' Williamson had joined Laphroaig distillery as a clerk in 1933, but in the 1940s as the owner succumbed to illness she found herself running the place and in 1950 became managing director, and eventually part owner. Not the first woman to manage a distillery business, an honour that may or may not reside with

'If I can annoy 90 per cent of the market and have 10 per cent that's alright with me'.

Elizabeth 'Bessie' Williamson joined Laphroaig distillery as a clerk in 1933, but in the 1940s as the owner succumbed to illness she found herself running the place and in 1950 became managing director, and eventually part owner. Not the first woman to manage a distillery business, she nonetheless blazed a trail for women in the industry in the 1960s, and as such was the subject of some considerable curiosity from the national media.

∧

Elizabeth Cumming of Cardhu, she nonetheless blazed a trail for women in the industry in the 1960s, and as such was the subject of some curiosity from the national media. Her contemporary, Gina MacKinnon, had taken control of the Drambuie business on the death of her husband in 1945, observing to her lawyer that 'I'm food for the sharks, but I'm ready'. Keeper of the secret of the whisky liqueur's famous recipe, allegedly handed down from Bonnie Prince Charlie, she was still making phials of the 'golden glowing liquid' to be blended with whisky and honey in the late 1960s, and still finding time to travel the world, principally the United States as an ambassador for the brand. 'The soft touch with the hard stuff' was how she and Bessie Williamson were profiled in *The Times* in 1967.

The 1970s and 1980s was a time when many Scotch distillers were trying to position themselves to develop a single malts business, shape-shifting from suppliers to blending houses to brand owners in their own right, not always an easy transition. Possibly the most spectacularly successful was Macallan, controlled by the Shiach family, descendants of the Victorian distillery entrepreneur Roderick Kemp, which had a distinguished reputation in the business as a blending malt, but no traction as a consumer brand. Into this picture came Edinburgh accountant Willie Phillips, who joined the company in 1974 and was rather surprised to become managing director four years later. It was Phillips, aided by 'marketing genius' Hugh Mitcalfe who transformed this unknown whisky into 'The Macallan, *The* Malt', winning Queen's Award for Exports in 1988. Phillips continued the Shiach strategy of laying down stocks for future aged bottlings (which other accountants might have baulked at) and also the focus on sherry cask maturation. He was an absolute stickler for quality. New markets were opened as Phillips and Mitcalfe both travelled the world on behalf of the brand, and also began to exploit the exceptional inventory in a series of hugely valuable and much sought-after limited releases, which few, if any Scotch

EVERYTHING YOU NEED TO KNOW ABOUT WHISKY

distillers had done. Some years after Phillips left Macallan following the change of ownership in 1996, Ken Grier deserted digestive biscuits and joined Edrington, taking over responsibility for the Macallan brand. An unusually high-profile marketing man, he set about another transformation, from 'The Macallan, *The Malt*' to 'Macallan the *Luxury* Malt' deploying both advertising, packaging, public relations and a much-accelerated limited-release programme aimed at collectors.

THE SPECIALISTS

As we've already seen, one of the triggers for the renaissance that Scotch has experienced since the 1990s was the growth of the specialist retail sector, not just in the UK, but all around the world with firms like La Maison du Whisky in France or Binny's in the United States. These businesses not only brought new products to the people, but also new personalities, not all of whom were versed in the traditional ways of whisky. Doing things the old-fashioned way were Elgin grocers Gordon & MacPhail, where George Urquhart, described in *Forbes* magazine as 'the godfather of single malt' had been quietly laying down whiskies, mostly from neighbouring Speyside distilleries, many owned by the DCL, since the 1950s. He introduced the 'Connoisseur's Choice' range in 1968, and his continuing legacy to his business, and to collectors, is all too evident to anyone privileged enough to visit the Gordon & MacPhail sample library. Someone who did it differently was Jack Milroy, an irrepressible wheeler-dealer entrepreneur whose Soho Wine Market (later the eponymous Milroy's) brought an increasing range of malt whiskies to the public, from four in 1969 to 140 in 1979 and over 600 in 1989. His brother Wallace, author of the *Whisky Almanac*, was responsible for sourcing many of these malts and also for persuading reluctant companies (particularly the DCL) to put them on the market. The brothers also started investing in casks that they would subsequently bottle and working with distillers to produce exclusive special releases, such as a single-cask Balvenie 50-year-old, sold to them in 1988 by Peter Gordon of William Grant at £150 and originally retailed at £360 a bottle. Waterford Distillery owner Mark Reynier was lucky enough to win a bottle in a charity auction, which claims Jack Milroy, converted him from wine to malt whisky. For the record, the bottle is now reckoned to be worth around £50,000 if you can find one. Today one of the largest specialist whisky retailers in the world is The Whisky Exchange, founded as an online business in 1999 by Sukhinder and Rajbir Singh. The brothers were born into the drinks business as their parents owned a small but very successful off-licence, The Nest, in Hanwell in West London. They took the difficult decision to sell the family business in 1998 and threw themselves at the mercy of the Internet and the growing number of whisky enthusiasts around the world who were looking for difficult-to-find bottles. In 2006 they opened their first shop in central London (where there are now three) and three years later staged the first Whisky Show in the capital, which at a stroke transformed the nature of live whisky events in the United Kingdom, and which both digitally and virtually is a magnet for whisky enthusiasts from all over the world. Over the years, in addition to developing their own Scotch whisky brands through Elixir Distillers, they have also championed the rise of Japanese and new world whiskies.

THE AWKWARD SQUAD

In 1978 Arthur J A Bell set up an innovative company called Scottish Direct to sell Scottish-craft products by direct mail and in between thimble clubs and tie clubs set up a business called 'The Whisky Connoisseur', selling miniatures and full-sized bottles of single malts from a wide range of distilleries to collectors around the UK and beyond. As an obituary wrote, he was 'quick-witted and incorrigibly mischievous, he delighted in debunking stereotypes and had an unerring gift for garnering publicity'. In 1985, following the acquisition of Arthur Bell and Sons by Guinness, 'J A' Bell produced the 'Gourmet Blend', a Scotch featuring a signature not entirely dissimilar from that on a standard bottle of Bell's. Easily provoked, badly advised and unable to see that they were walking into an ambush, Guinness brought the full force of the law against him, only to suffer humiliation in Edinburgh's Court of Session when the verdict was found in 'J A' Bell's favour, the judge uttering the memorable words, 'a man has an inalienable right to trade under his own name'. An industry like Scotch whisky needs to have an awkward squad, the square pegs who delight in not fitting into the round hole predestined for them. Peter Mackie, founder of the White Horse brand, was one, driving the Dewars and Buchanans to distraction with his contrariness; he has more recent counterparts. Take Richard Joynson, famously described by Charlie MacLean as 'a former fish', who with his wife Lindsay set up Loch Fyne Whiskies in 1993 in the main street of Inveraray, Argyll. Joynson spoke to the world from his small shop in the middle of nowhere through his regular mailshots and increasingly the Internet. He also produced the Scotch Whisky Review, a mixture of useful whisky-related information for customers, thoughtful writing, and opinionated rants, showing no mercy to those producers and bottlers alike who had provoked his righteous ire. This was something very new in an industry normally awash with self-love, and was not only enjoyed by consumers, but secretly adored by many in the business. His shop became another whisky mecca on the increasingly well-trodden road to Campbeltown and Islay for whisky fans from all over the globe.

Hardly surprising then that Joynson was such a great fan of self-styled whisky maverick Mark Reynier, who you may remember, having won a bottle of Jack and Wallace Millroy's 50-year-old Balvenie in a charity auction decided to turn his back on the wine trade and embrace Scotch instead. Like an overexcited schoolboy with a stick, there wasn't anyone who Reynier didn't poke several times on the road to successfully putting Bruichladdich firmly among the malt enthusiast's favourite brands. Adroitly deploying the marketing and PR techniques that he lambasted the 'big players' for using, and never failing to miss an opportunity to get some senior whisky executive hot under the collar, he was an unstoppable force of nature, until that is, his backers decided they had had enough fun and sold up the business to the French. Islay's loss has been Waterford's gain, where Reynier has converted a former Diageo brewery into a distillery where he is producing terroir-driven whiskies, to the delight of some and the bemusement of others. Equally happy to get under the skin of well-known companies was Phillip, or Pip, Hills, who can be credited for starting what is now one of the largest whisky clubs in the world, The Scotch Malt Whisky Society, and for sparking the interest in single cask whiskies. Hills had begun clubbing together with friends to buy odd casks of single malt for their own enjoyment, but the idea grew like Topsy. Hills was firmly in the tradition of the old school of literary whisky Golden Agers, and as Reynier would do later, never failed to take a pop at the whisky establishment when the chance presented itself. *Scots on Scotch*, the book he edited in 1991, was a manifesto from a list of distinguished contributors, for a Scotch whisky revolution. Similarly important in the growth of interest in single cask whiskies, and equally uncompromising, is Andrew Symington of Signatory Whiskies, and now the owner of Edradour distillery in Perthshire. Symington has a barely constrained passion for Scotch, and for doing things the 'old-fashioned way' when it comes to his distillery (he is the man with the archaic Morton's Refrigerator, see page 18). He was, and is, a hands-on business owner with little respect for hierarchies, something underlined by the boiler suit that he always used to wear at whisky shows. And, as anyone will tell you, few take as much delight and pleasure in the joys and companionship of his product than him.

The Whisky Evangelists, left to right: Richard Paterson OBE, Dr Bill Lumsden, Jim McEwan, Bill Samuels, Fred Noe.

The Awkward Squad, left to right: Richard Joynson, Arthur J A Bell, Mark Reynier, Andrew Symington.

>

EVERYTHING YOU NEED TO KNOW ABOUT WHISKY

WHISKY EVANGELISTS

VS

AWKWARD SQUAD

IT'S ONLY ROCK AND ROLL ...

It was almost as if the whisky industry had been trying to keep its own personalities under lock and key for decades. The malts evangelists such as Grant's or the Macallan had learned very quickly how important it was to put a face to a brand but larger companies, particularly United Distillers (now Diageo), feared the potentially disruptive influence that powerful public personalities could have in such organisations. True industry giants like Ronnie Martin OBE and Turnbull Hutton, production directors as the DCL morphed into Diageo, were kept hidden from view, in the latter's case possibly because he possessed a vocabulary that would make a trooper blush. There was still a deep culture of secrecy to be dealt with. Smart suited and occasionally kilted, superannuated sales and marketing executives were hired to fly the flag for Dewar's and Buchanan's but from under the radar Evan Cattanach, manager at Cardhu distillery, emerged as one of the first whisky celebrities, literally serenading audiences around the world on behalf of his own brand and Johnnie Walker. Cattanach was the first of many as distillery managers and blenders were put on the road to take their product to the people, who welcomed them with unrestrained adoration. The rock-star triumvirate of Richard Paterson OBE, Dr Bill Lumsden and Jim McEwan became regular fixtures on an ever-growing circuit of whisky shows, consumer tastings, trade visits and media events to promote their brands, developing a very particular style of whisky showmanship. Not to everyone's taste, and sometimes more suited to a seaside variety theatre rather than Scotch whisky, these three (and others) were nonetheless responsible for generating a huge amount of interest in single malt Scotch in particular and winning the hearts, and more importantly the minds and pockets, of consumers around the world. Their contribution to the growth of single malts simply cannot be overstated. They had counterparts too in the world of other whiskies: Barry Crockett who in addition to being one of the brains behind the Irish-Distiller's-led pot still whisky renaissance, was also the face of Midleton and Jameson, and Colm Egan, Bushmills distiller with a handy line in tales and toasts. Fred Noe, the grandson of Jim Beam, both distiller and brand ambassador for the family brand; Bill Samuels who drove the success of Maker's Mark in the early years and Jimmy Russell, who was responsible for the making of Wild Turkey for over fifty years. In the eyes of the whisky-drinking public, they all came to personify their brands as they travelled and talked. At the same time, the demand for personal appearances began to impinge seriously on their regular jobs – who was making the whisky, finishing the finishes or blending the blends? As a result, the whisky brand ambassador was born, to take the weight off the professionals and transfer it instead to the generous expense and air miles accounts of these aspiring Scotch whisky entertainers and educators. An unusual example is Ashok Chokalingam, who for many years was the sole representative for Amrut – and quality Indian whisky – around the world, not just looking after all sales and brand ambassadorial duties with indefatigable enthusiasm in the face of significant cynicism, but also, it seemed, running their whole international business with an infectious personality and honesty. The award-winning Angela D'Orazio, who joined the whisky world as a Glenmorangie brand ambassador in Sweden, joined Mackmyra Svensk Whisky as master blender and global brand ambassador in 2004, since then she has helped build the reputation of the brand in many established whisky markets, and is today their 'Chief Nosing Officer'.

Women occupy some of the most senior executive roles in today's whisky industry, and they can be found in the production side of the industry from apprentice coppersmiths to distillers. While there are some very prominent female brand ambassadors, the world of whisky blending tends to be one where women not only feature strongly, but are also very visible to the whisky-drinking public. Maureen Robinson joined the Distillers

Company in 1977 as a bench scientist before taking on a role in quality assurance, which led her into the blending room. She works on both single malts and blends, having been responsible both for the development of the Singleton range of whiskies and the famous Rare Malts and early special releases. She has also worked as blender on the Buchanan range of whiskies; as such she is well known to consumers in Latin America, while she has travelled extensively in Asia to support her malts work. Her equivalent in Canadian Whisky would be Joanna Scandella, the equally time-served blender of Crown Royal. Similarly well travelled is Dr Rachel Barrie, now responsible for the Scotch whiskies of Brown Forman such as GlenDronach and Glenglassaugh, a well-known industry figure who is also known for her work with Glenmorangie and Morrison Bowmore. While women have been occupying managerial roles in distilling for thirty years or more, only a few have become well known to the whisky-drinking public, the most notable probably being Georgie Crawford, a native Ileach who started her whisky career at the Scotch Malt Whisky Society before joining Diageo. Having trained as a distillery manager, she has famously worked at Lagavulin and Port Ellen maltings, and was leading the project to rebuild Port Ellen distillery. She has recently joined Elixir Distillers and will be the manager at their new distillery now under construction outside Port Ellen village. A fixture on the Islay distilling scene Georgie is not only known to those Islay whisky fans who travel to the island each year but also to the many she has met on her travels around the world. Working not far from Crawford, Jackie Thomson has become the face of Ardbeg to its many devotees around the world. In hosting visitors and running tastings and special events, Jackie has become synonymous with the brand; she's been at the distillery since it was reopened in 1997 and has undoubtedly made a major contribution to its success, and to the development of that very particular sort of loyalty that Ardbeg fans display.

THE MOST IMPORTANT PERSON?

We asked our whisky insiders who they thought was the most influential person on the industry over the past thirty years, and from the past. Aeneas Coffey was prominent in the former: 'for gifting us with the means to create a lighter style of grain spirit,' said Becky Paskin, without which 'Scotch may not have become the global powerhouse it is today'. Many agreed. Alfred Barnard, for the insights he gave us into distilling in the past was another popular choice. Tommy Dewar, W H Ross and Samuel Bronfman also got mentioned for their role in shaping today's industry, as did Charles Doig, chosen by Rob Allanson, the distillery architect and 'inventor' of his eponymous 'ventilator', or the pagoda-topped kilns that have come to define the shape of many distilleries all around the world. Ingvar Ronde wasn't the only person to mention Andrew Volstead 'who initiated the Prohibition, which had a huge impact on the popularity of Scotch in the USA'. Both Sukhinder Singh and Isabel Graham-Yooll opted for Jack and Wallace Milroy. When it came to the most influential person over the past thirty years, there were a couple of strong preferences. The first was the late Dr Jim Swan, described by Becky Paskin as 'the godfather of new world whisky'. Swan was a consultant to numerous new distilleries over the past twenty years or more: 'for good or ill', said Billy Abbott, 'he has not only helped lots of producers to start making whisky, but also created a new style, focused around young whisky that develops the characteristic flavours of ageing faster than it might otherwise have done'. The other leading choice was Serge Valentin for his unique contribution to the growth of interest in single malts. The ever-thoughtful Richard Woodard provocatively opted for 'the consumer'. We all sometimes get the past and the present slightly muddled, and so it was with our insiders, for in the answers we were given one person straddled both like a giant, his contribution to the popularity of Scotch whisky, and whiskies around the world through his writing and public appearances being without compare. That was the timeless Michael Jackson.

Index

Index

ACKNOWLEDGEMENTS

In addition to Sukhinder Singh and Chris Maybin at The Whisky Exchange, and Camilla Ackley at Ebury Publishing, I would like to thank the following friends and colleagues who have, knowingly or not, helped in the writing of this book: Billy Abbott, Rob Allanson, Gillian Bell, Karen Bennett, Jim Beveridge, Chantal Bristow, Dave Broom, Jim Brown, Neil Cochrane, Emmanuel Dron, Andrew Ford, Isabel Graham-Yooll, Monique Huston (for the Vienna Beef sausage story), Ailana Kamelmacher, Davin de Kergommeaux, Keith Law, Charlie MacLean, Kurt Maitland, Rachel McCormack, Annabel Meikle, Jack Milroy, Mike Nicolson, Alessandro Palazzi, Becky Paskin, Maureen Robertson, Patrick Roberts, Ingvar Ronde, Sam Simmons, Bernhard Schäfer, Serge Valentin, Richard Woodard, Hideo Yamaoka. Written during lockdown, I would have struggled to complete this book without the various digital resources provided particularly by the British Library, the National Library of Scotland, and the London Library. I have an abiding debt to the Diageo Archive and the very professional team of archivists there. You can't write a whisky book without enjoying some of Scotland's midnight wine on the way, so particular thanks go to John Johnston, Hector Henderson, Hugh and Kenneth MacAskill, George Granville Leveson-Gower (Marquis of Stafford and first Duke of Sutherland), and, of course, John Walker.

— Nicholas Morgan, April 2021

I

Published in 2021 by Ebury Press an imprint of Ebury Publishing,
20 Vauxhall Bridge Road,
London SW1V 2SA

Ebury Press is part of the Penguin Random House group of companies
whose addresses can be found at global.penguinrandomhouse.com

Text © Speciality Drinks Limited 2021
Illustrations © Jonny Wan 2021
Design © Studio Polka 2021

Editor: Camilla Ackley
Production: Sian Pratley

This edition first published by Ebury Press in 2021

www.penguin.co.uk

A CIP catalogue record for this book is available from the British Library

ISBN 9781529108750

Printed and bound: TBB, a.s. Slovakia

The authorised representative in the EEA is Penguin Random House Ireland, Morrison
Chambers, 32 Nassau Street, Dublin D02 YH68.

Penguin Random House is committed to a sustainable future for our business, our readers
and our planet. This book is made from Forest Stewardship Council® certified paper.